CAPTAIN WILLIAM
BLIGH
an illustrated history

Published by Paul Hamlyn Pty. Ltd.,
176 South Creek Road,
Dee Why West, N.S.W., Australia, 2099.
© Copyright Paul Hamlyn Pty. Ltd., 1972.
First Published 1972.
Printed in Singapore.
Designed by Hugh McLeod.
ISBN 0 600 07060 3

CAPTAIN WILLIAM
BLIGH

by Philip Weate
& Caroline Graham

Paul Hamlyn
Sydney, London, New York, Toronto

Foreword

The eventful historiography of Bligh. This, in itself a fascinating story, is an appropriate and even necessary introduction. Any interpretation of Bligh must be partly subjective because his reputation in his lifetime was overlaid with all the emotion and propaganda arising from the successive trials and courts martial which dogged him throughout a stormy naval career. It has been difficult for historians to separate objective fact from propaganda in Bligh's case —controversy still exists and perhaps the ghost of the abrasive Bligh will never be laid to rest. The problem is such that only one 'definitive' biography of Bligh has been written, by George Mackaness, as far back as 1931. This is largely sympathetic, though the popular image of Bligh—boosted by Hollywood—has been that of a blustering tyrant. In 1937 Dr H. V. Evatt's *Rum Rebellion* was published, supporting Bligh's actions against Macarthur and the Rum Corps in New South Wales—an interpretation which was challenged in the late fifties by the biographer and historian, M. H. Ellis. This resulted in 'The Great "Rum Rebellion" Debate', involving many Australian historians, which was carried on in the pages of various Australian journals for several years and was never satisfactorily concluded, though it provoked libellous personal attacks and—according to Ellis—anonymous threats of violence. Interest was added to the debate by

the fact that one of Ellis' earlier major biographies, *Lachlan Macquarie,* had been sympathetic towards Bligh, but in writing his 'John Macarthur' his opinion of Bligh underwent a radical change.

The fundamental question, never to be solved apparently, is this: Was Bligh's violent temper and stubborn nature such that the mutiny on the *Bounty* and the Rum Rebellion were made almost inevitable? Or was he rather the victim of circumstances which would have been beyond the control of even the most diplomatic and temperate commander or governor? The evidence inclines towards the latter view— and yet there is no doubt that Bligh, himself a superman in matters of efficiency and endurance, was infuriated too easily with laziness, carelessness and insubordination in others. Letters show how tenderly he loved his wife and daughters—and they him—yet he would have been a difficult man to serve under in any capacity. What one thinks of Bligh ultimately depends not only on a knowledge of general conditions and expectations within the British Navy in the late 18th century, and a knowledge of the state of affairs in New South Wales, but on one's own attitude to those who, endowed with super-abundant energy and a need for constant action, cannot help treading on the toes of those about them... and Bligh, in this respect, was elephantine.

Contents

CHAPTER J

Early life at Plymouth

Only a few details of William Bligh's early life remain, but enough is known about his family and environment to give a rough sketch of his development. His parents, Francis and Jane, were married in 1753, and he was born on September 9, 1754, as far as is known, their only child.

The Blighs were an ancient Cornish family. Their name appeared in the Domesday Book, and four Blighs were Mayors of Bodmin between 1505 and 1588. An off-shoot of the Bodmin clan moved to St Tudy parish in 1680, when a John Bligh acquired the Manor of Tinten, which was held by his descendants as late as 1817. Francis Bligh was born there in 1721, the fifth son of Richard Bligh. He later moved to nearby Plymouth to enter the service of H M Customs. During the course of his long career as customs officer he married three times, and, it is reported, had a dashing carriage with yellow wheels which was a well-known sight in the streets of Plymouth.

Little is known of his first wife, William Bligh's mother. At the time of their marriage she was a widow—a Mrs Jane Pearce, nee Bond. She was forty or forty-one years old; Francis was about nine years her junior. By her first marriage she had a daughter, Catherine, who married her cousin John Bond, a naval surgeon. The Bligh family bible records the birth of a number of children to John and Catherine, and since John Bond's career constantly took him away from home, it is possible that the two families lived together at Francis Bligh's house. Anyway, throughout his life William Bligh maintained a close relationship with the Bonds and their children, who were several years younger than himself.

When Bligh was born, there was still much significance in being a Cornishman. Though he was brought up in a cosmopolitan port on the Devonshire side of the Tamar River, many old Cornish families had their 'Plymouth branch' and no doubt the Blighs moved in a circle of fellow countrymen.

The Cornish still regarded the English as foreigners, and vice versa. Cornwall preserved its Celtic culture, and, in the far west, English was still not spoken. The county was not easily accessible, and in the mid-eighteenth century the sight of a coach was rare. The people were poor and rebellious. Tin-mining, often dominated by 'foreigners', had turned some areas into the most densely populated parts of England, but conditions in the mines were appalling and wages pitiful. Miners sought oblivion in gin, and often turned violent when drunk or angry. Corn shortages caused food riots—then the miners 'ravaged up and down the country in a very insolent manner' plundering 'mowhays, barns and cellars'. The Cornish gentry and rising middle classes lived in constant fear of a general insurrection, and perhaps this fear of the lower classes lay behind William Bligh's overbearing manner.

The Cornish gentry no longer made gestures of independence, but were at best passive to British rule. They connived with the lower classes or turned a blind eye to the traditional Cornish practices of 'wrecking' and smuggling. Bligh's father, Francis, was probably no exception in his capacity as H M Customs Officer at Plymouth.

In Bligh's time the huge quantities of brandy and tea smuggled into Cornwall cost the English Exchequer about £150,000 a year. Cornishmen obviously felt little loyalty to the British rulers.

So, although William Bligh served in the British Navy, high-minded patriotism was probably not his strongest motivation. He was a true professional—the navy was not, for him, invested with a 'band of brothers' mystique, but was the institution which allowed him to prove himself and provide his family with a good living.

Bligh was always eager for the perquisites of office, though so were most English officers, since basic salaries were not good. If, true to Cornish custom, he sometimes managed to stretch English regulations a little his way, so did many English officers when the chance arose.

William Bligh's childhood at Plymouth was an exciting one. The port was swarming with spies, saboteurs and smugglers, and was host to a flood of prisoners of war after the short peace in 1748 (War of Austrian Succession). Attempts at sabotaging the great dockyards never ceased. Prisoners from various wars, herded in foul quarters, made constant attempts to escape. Plymouth was also chief port for the entire hierarchy of British seadogs —Grenville, Frobisher, Raleigh, Drake and Hawkins.

As larger ships were built, the docks were dug to accommodate them, and Plymouth soon became one of the busiest ports in the world. The wars brought a turbulent era of recruiting, pressing and ship-building; attracting crowds of adventurers and camp-followers. All the admirals frequented the city, and many military expeditions were mounted there. William Bligh, as a boy of 14, may have watched Captain Cook sail out of the Sound on his circumnavigation in 1768. Or he may have seen Lord Anson sailing proudly up the Sound after one of his victories over the French.

The great 'first raters', the queen ships of the navy, towering walls of wood carrying their complement of 800 men and more, were an exciting sight for the children of Plymouth. Bligh probably felt as did his contemporary, Byam Martin, who saw his first 'first rater'— the old *Royal George*—at the age of seven: 'I was so rooted to the spot, so perfectly motionless . . . so absorbed in wonder that I should have been there the whole day if they had not sent one of the boat's crew to fetch me down . . . Ye gods! What a sight! What a sensation! I feel it now as I write and if I live to the age of Methuselah it will remain unimpaired. It is impossible to forget the astonishment and delight with which my eyes were fixed upon this ship. Nothing so exquisitely touching has occurred to me since to produce the same frantic joy. I remember old John Allen said "I see, sir, you are already determined to be a sailor". He never spoke a truer word . . .'

William Bligh's parents had decided on a naval career for their son while he was still a small boy. He was lucky in having the two most important qualifications for becoming a sea officer in the 18th century: he was born a 'gentleman', with parents who could provide him with an allowance; young gentlemen afloat received no pay to start with, but were expected to live up to their status. And the Blighs of St Tudy, some of whom had been naval officers, commanded a modest amount of useful 'Interest' in naval matters, i.e., personal influence.

The stepping-stones to high naval rank were outwardly straightforward.

The elite of the navy were those grades which held the King's Commission. In descending order of seniority and salary these were flag-officers; the admirals, vice-admirals and rear-admirals; captains, commanders and lieutenants. So step number one was to become eligible for your commission, which you did by passing your lieutenant's examination after six years of service at sea. Two of these years had to be spent as a midshipman or as master's mate, and you had to be at least 20 years old. Once you had

received the commission the first professional hurdle was over, but you would be most eager to press on, because a lieutenant's life was a hard one, on a basic salary of not much more than £100 a year. In view of the discomforts, dangers and responsibilities, this was inadequate. But the captain of a first-rate ship got about £802. So the next step, and perhaps the most vital one, was to win your promotion or 'posting' to the rank of captain, after gaining some necessary experience as commander of small 'non-post' ships. Once a post captain, the hardest part of the navy game was over, for, as long as you avoided really scandalous mishaps, you were from now on promoted automatically up the ladder and through the ranks as your seniors died off. The King himself could not alter your place on the ladder, and to reach the very top rung—Admiral of the Fleet—you only had to live longer than everyone else.

However, the navy, like all 18th century institutions, was extremely corrupt and there were numerous loop-holes in the system. The system was quite openly abused by the ambitious. For instance, if you were not made a post captain early in life, you had little hope of becoming an admiral before you died, so it was important to get a head start on your fellows. The minimum age at which you could begin your initial six years of training was supposed to be 13 (or 11, if your father was a naval officer). But this limit was widely ignored. It was easy to give a false age in those days before compulsory registration of birth, and it was common for boys to go to sea at the age of nine or younger. If your father was an officer, so much the better —one Daniel Woodriff went to sea, rated as lieutenant's servant, when two years old, and accompanied his father around the world at the age of five. After two years at sea these children could officially be rated midshipmen—as naval historian Michael Lewis says, 'It was not uncommon, therefore, for midshipmen . . . to suck their thumbs'.

So, around the age of 15, many boys had six years of service under their belt and could sit for their lieutenant's examination. At this point, a birth certificate was actually demanded to prove that they were 20. But this was easily forged—often, the story goes, by the porter in the hall where the young gentlemen presented themselves for examination.

If parents feared to send their tiny sons to sea, a naval career was still possible.

The Section of a First Rate Ship of War, Shewing its var

A 1st rate warship such as could be seen at Plymouth when Bligh was a child.

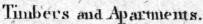

Timbers and Apartments.

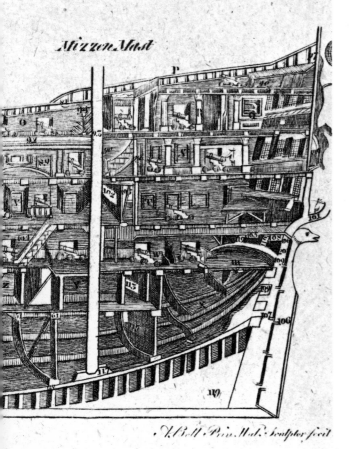

Above and below decks of a first rate ship of war of the late 18th century. Majestic to see, they broke the bodies of the men who had to manage them.

11

A captain would simply enter the name of the young protégé on the ship's books without taking him to sea at all. Thus a boy could chalk up six years of 'book time' without putting a foot on a deck. He could not become a lieutenant immediately—too dangerous for his shipmates—but he might be rated midshipman on his first real voyage, a short cut of at least two years.

The loop-holes in the system meant that the amount of Interest your family could command was the prime factor in rapid promotion. Interest was simply the pulling of strings through a web of family and political connections.

To begin with, your family needed Interest in order to find a captain to take you to sea. This was the only way to get on board as a young gentleman (prospective officer) unless you were one of the very few graduates from an unpopular naval college. After that, Interest was used as widely as possible to obtain your first commission and then to have you made 'post'.

Interest and bribery by no means always succeeded, since there were so many playing at the game. Lady Nelson mentioned one failure in a letter written in 1797. She referred to George Tobin, the son of a West Indies merchant, who had sailed with Bligh as a lieutenant in 1790. Seven years later, life was passing him by and he still had not been made a post captain. Lady Nelson remarked haughtily: 'George Tobin still a lieutenant. All Mr Tobin's expensive presents to some lords and ladies and captains cannot get him made.' Cruder forms of bribery were apparently not uncommon. A wealthy gentleman wrote in 1764, to his younger brother who, like Tobin, was angling for his 'post': 'If any sum of money should be necessary for it, for I have heard there are sometimes bargains of that sort, I will answer any draft that you might find it necessary to draw . . . I am so very anxious to have you made post, that I would omit no possible means, and I think you could not lay out a sum of money to greater advantage'.

First class Interest was far more desirable than bribery. An excellent illustration of this level of Interest at work is recorded in a conversation in 1794 between a Lord Hawke and the 14-year-old son of a friend: 'When there is a general naval promotion,' said the former, 'I am always allowed to provide for one friend, to get him made either a lieutenant, a commander or a post captain, therefore when your time is up, let me know, and you shall be my lieutenant. In short, you are as sure of the commission as if you had it in your pocket.' Some really expert and influential families managed to have sons posted at the incredibly early age of 17, so that they reached flag-officer rank long before they were in their dotage. But usually the game required perseverance and finesse.

The pastoral outskirts of Plymouth in the mid 18th century. William Bligh, born September 1754, spent his boyhood in Plymouth where his father was a customs officer.

A Lieutenant Dillon described his strategy in 1803: 'I sketched out a statement of my services . . . Lord Melville was then head of the Admiralty. I referred his Lordship to my friend Lord Gambier. But previous to closing my dispatch, I thought I should do right by showing it to my two influential friends Lord Yarmouth and Colonel Abercromby. . . . The latter expressed himself very warmly in my favour . . . "I think", said he, "I can settle that matter for you. My brother has married Lord Melville's daughter".' In 1763, a loving mother, Countess Cornwallis, wrote to her son to let him know how hard she was trying: 'As soon as I heard Admiral [Sir William] Barnaby had kissed hands for the command of the West India squadron . . . I wrote to Miss Ottley, whose aunt he married . . . the Monday following Mr Ottley brought Sir William to me, who expressed great civility . . . You may imagine I did not omit the giving him to understand post was the favour we wanted.'

The Blighs of St Tudy were not able to wield Interest on a level with the peerage. Yet Bligh collected enough Interest to short-circuit weary years on low pay suffered, for instance, by men of exceptional ability but humble origins like Captain Cook. Cook was competent enough to be one of the rare examples of men who rose from lower deck to quarter deck status. However, he did not receive his commission until he was 40, and was promoted post captain only three years before his death.

Bligh's parents found an obliging captain who entered their son's name in the books of HMS *Monmouth* on July 1, 1762, when he was seven years old, for a period of seven months. Bligh survived to reach the rank of vice-admiral—his intelligence, skill and energy helped to make up for lack of first class Interest, though his promotion was far from rapid.

The next seven years of Bligh's life are a blank. He may have attended school at Plymouth, or he may have gone to sea, where he would have been tutored by school masters employed for the benefit of young gentlemen afloat. Sea-going teachers had low wages and low status on board, and the hard life, in an atmosphere not conducive to learning, attracted only the dregs of the profession—largely alcoholics and eccentrics who found service at sea their only available livelihood. Some-how or other Bligh apparently received an education well above average.

A view of Plymouth Harbour in the early 19th century. The artist, C. Stanfield, gives a good impression of the immense size the warships had reached.

CHAPTER 11

Learning with Captain Cook

that the various plants and animals he had left were flourishing.

Now this voyage with Cook on the *Resolution* took Bligh to two places which were to become focal points in the drama of his career. Head winds prevented Cook from laying Tahiti direct, so he took the next best course and made for the Friendly Islands. It was in this group, near Tofua, that the mutiny took place on the *Bounty.* Here, too, Bligh and the 'loyalists' cast adrift on the launch, narrowly escaped massacre.

After three months at Tonga, where the Polynesians enthusiastically stole tools, muskets, a quadrant and all Captain Clerke's cats, they arrived at Tahiti on August 12. There is no account of Bligh's reaction to these magical islands which later were to undermine the discipline and loyalty of his own crew. Cook's stay in Tahiti was shorter than the *Bounty's,* but, even so, two of the *Discovery's* crew deserted at Raiatea. They were found after a long search.

Six weeks were spent there, and then the

two ships set sail northwards on the important business of the voyage. On January 18, 1778, two high islands of the Hawaiian group were sighted. Cook was amazed that Polynesians lived so far north, but, anxious to make the most of the northern summer for his arctic exploration, he stopped only briefly.

Through stormy and difficult seas, they reached Nootka Sound on Vancouver Island. Bligh charted the Sound, and Cook named an island after him. Repairs were made to the *Resolution's* mizzen mast, and they sailed north again, carefully skirting the Alaskan coast. Then through Bering Strait to latitude 70°6′ N. where 'the further progress of the ships northwards was rendered impossible by ice extending from Continent to Continent'.

Exploration was continued on the Asian coast for a few weeks, with Bligh busily charting and the men grumbling that the fresh walrus meat, which Cook tried to persuade them to eat, made them sick.

With the approach of winter, they turned south for the Hawaiian group, which they sighted again on November 26, 1778. Bligh charted and surveyed the whole of the chain, then named by Cook the 'Sandwich Islands'. It was his melancholy honour to have surveyed and selected an anchorage on Hawaii, Kealakekua Bay, where Cook was killed.

Resolution by Henry Roberts, a midshipman on the third voyage who redrew most of Bligh's charts for publication. Bligh was furious that Robert's copy of his plan of the Sandwich Islands did not show the mountains accurately.

A portrait of Captain James Cook as Bligh may have known him during the third voyage. Engraving by John Basire after William Hodges, 1777.

John Webber, official artist on the third Cook voyage, by J. D. Mottet.

Cook's plan was to rest there and overhaul the ships after the hard season in the north. The Hawaiians welcomed them enthusiastically, and Cook was at once the recipient of divine honours. He was given the use of a sacred enclosure, or 'heiau' for his tents; officers and men wandered and explored in perfect safety. The islanders traded their food and goods at a very favourable rate; the only annoyance to Cook was once again the Polynesian expertise in thievery.

After nearly three weeks, however, some tension developed. The 180 British men were large eaters, and the supply of provisions was not nearly so lavish by the time Cook sailed on February 4, 1779. When a strong gale cracked the *Resolution's* mainmast, Cook returned to Kealakekua with reluctance, knowing they had outworn their welcome.

The carpenters hurried to repair the mast on the beach. Then the *Discovery's* cutter was stolen, and Cook ordered a blockade of the bay, and went ashore with a small party of marines to take the King of the island hostage until the cutter was returned. They were on the beach with the King, surrounded by a great crowd of Hawaiians, when shots were heard from the south side of the bay. Almost immediately news came that a young chief had been killed. The crowd grew hostile and a furious hail of stones was directed at Cook's party. A volley from the marines checked the attack, but, as Cook turned to signal his boats to come closer, a priest felled him with a club and the Hawaiians surged forward and stabbed him to death.

Later, apparently shocked by what they had done, the Hawaiians mourned and honoured Cook, and they asked his men, 'When will the god—when will Erono—come again?'

After further skirmishes, in which Bligh played a valiant part, a truce was declared and Cook's body was recovered, to be given a sea burial. On February 23 they set sail again, with the ailing Captain Clerke now in command. Bligh recorded that the burden of managing the ships fell on him, though there is no other evidence for this assertion.

Another voyage was made to the Arctic Sea, this time probing to the west after passing through Bering Strait. On turning back, two days out of Petropavlovsk, Captain Clerke died (August 22, 1779), increasing Bligh's responsibilities.

The *Resolution* and the *Endeavour* anchored in Snug Corner, Prince William Sound, Alaska, 1778, on their way north to Bering Strait. Bligh explored one arm of the Sound for Cook. By William Ellis.

North of the Bering Strait the *Resolution* beating through
the ice with the *Discovery* in the distance in danger
of being trapped. By Webber.

He charted Macao and Typa on their way homewards via the Cape of Good Hope. They reached the Nore on October 4, 1780. They had been away for over four years, and in that time only one man had died from scurvy. This alone was no small triumph—all seamen remembered Lord Anson's circumnavigation, on which 1,051 men had died out of the 1,955 who embarked.

For Bligh, this time with Cook was a wonderful apprenticeship; four years going from latitude 50° South to 70° North. But in spite of Cook's confidence in him, and the beautiful quality of his chart work, Bligh was one of the few who did not receive immediate promotion. Perhaps his vanity and professional jealously had alienated those who remained in command. When he received a published copy of Cook's Third Voyage four years later, he wrote belittling comments about Captain King and other officers in the margin, and was infuriated that his charts were attributed to Lieutenant Roberts, master's mate in the *Resolution,* a grievance which he still harped upon 11 years later.

Yet Bligh could go out of his way to be kindly & considerate—at least when his competitive spirit was not aroused. Young Midshipman Trevenen wrote that when he was in the depths of depression, 'two friendly hands were reached out, & saved me from the gulph into which I was plunging, & if ever I get any promotion in the service, which Ambition bids me hope, I shall always gratefully acknowledge that it is totally owing to Capt. King & Mr Bligh our master; they took notice of me, & offered me the use of their cabins & advice'.

Captain Cook's landing place, Norfolk Island.

Webber's unfinished drawing of Hawaiians dancing. The discs are feather shields.

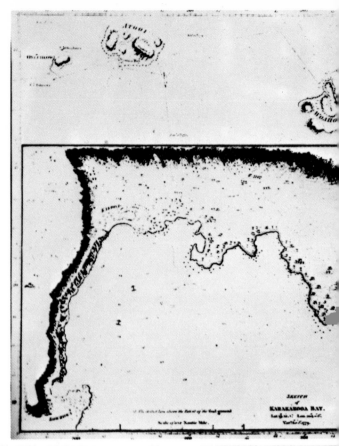

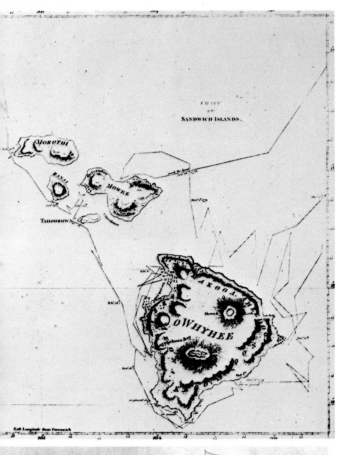

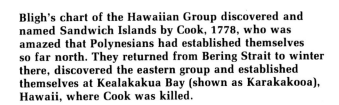

Bligh's chart of the Hawaiian Group discovered and named Sandwich Islands by Cook, 1778, who was amazed that Polynesians had established themselves so far north. They returned from Bering Strait to winter there, discovered the eastern group and established themselves at Kealakakua Bay (shown as Karakakooa), Hawaii, where Cook was killed.

The death of Cook, February 1779, by John Cleveley who sailed in the *Adventure* on Cook's second voyage. Cleveley developed this aquatint from a sketch by his brother James who was a carpenter in the *Resolution.*

CHAPTER 111

Bligh in the West Indies

Bligh had shown great concern for his family in his letters to them. He wrote to John Bond, his half-sister's husband, offering their son Francis 'to accept of his schooling at Latin, as it's a present I intended for him before I wrote to you last, and have been very sorry I then forgot to mention it'. When he was paid off at the end of 1780, he was out of active service for some months, and probably visited his family in Plymouth. Then he went off on a holiday tour round the west of England, to the Orkneys, and the Isle of Man.

In the city of Douglas on the Isle of Man he had the good fortune to meet a delightful, cultured and unattached woman, Elizabeth Betham. She was the daughter of Richard Betham of Glasgow, a government official on the island, and a scholar who numbered Adam Smith, Principal Robertson and David Hume amongst his good friends—Edinburgh intellectuals from the golden age when the Scottish capital was called 'the Academy of Europe'.

Elizabeth was then 27, two years older than William Bligh. Life among the Manxmen was probably dull, and Bligh, with his stories of adventure in the South Seas, must have seemed an interesting proposition. Anyway, the two were married at Douglas on February 4, 1781. Mrs Bligh smiles vivaciously from her portrait, under a halo of dark, glossy curls; one small hand resting on her lap dog; the other sybaritically dangling a luscious bunch of grapes in keeping with the fashion of the day—no provincial lass here, she tells us. Lucky Bligh: his 'dear, dear Betsy' was to serve his interests actively and loyally; fighting lonely battles in his absence against those who sought to slander her 'Mr Bligh' until at last, 'her nerves being very much broke', she died, but that was 30 years hence.

Their honeymoon was brief, for on February 14, Bligh was back in service as master of the frigate *Belle Poule,* leaving Elizabeth in their lodgings in Douglas. In August, he was 'blooded', in his first sea battle, with a Dutch fleet while on escort duty with a merchant convoy going from the Baltic to England. Perhaps as a result of good conduct, he now received his commission at last, and was appointed to a larger ship as fifth-lieutenant.

After serving as lieutenant for several months, he was in a position to angle for his first command, the next step towards being posted. Marriage had given him new influence in the form of his wife's uncle, Duncan Campbell, an important West Indies trader, plantation and ship owner. On Campbell's advice, he recommended himself to a Campbell kinsman who was a vice-admiral, but this canny move was completely unsuccessful. He remained a lowly lieutenant, played a part in the relief of Gibraltar in 1783, and arrived home to the Isle of Man the day before the birth of his second child, Mary.

Their first daughter, Harriet Maria, was born in 1782, and Elizabeth may have taken the new baby to see its father during one of his brief leaves, for Bligh had written to Duncan Campbell in April: 'I heard today from Mrs Bligh who is now at the Isle of Man and very well as is the family there. The Voyage being rough they suffered sea sickness for nine hours and the child had only sailors to nurse it, the servants being exceedingly ill'. That is the first hint we have of Mrs Bligh's dislike of the sea, which was to become almost obsessive, preventing her from travelling to New South Wales with Bligh to take up her position as Governor's Lady. It was a most significant phobia, for her presence there might have mellowed Bligh, perhaps altering the course of the colony's history.

The American War of Independence was over by the end of 1782, and the navy was reduced to a peace-time skeleton. Bligh and many others were put on half-pay, which, for a lieutenant, was a paltry two shillings a day. For some months the family were together again in Douglas, living quietly. 'Mrs Bligh's father and sister, Mrs Colden, we go to see two or three times a week, and one or two friends who we spend an hour with now and then, but otherwise I remain at home and as I can get plenty of Books, improve myself that way.' Bligh complained of the high cost of provisions, and, though always a moderate drinker, wrote rather wistfully, 'I do not taste a spoonful of Spirits from one end of the week to the other'. Then Duncan Campbell offered him a command in the West India merchant trade. Before he left, he was able to move the family out of their lodgings and into 'one of the neatest Houses in Town for eight guineas a year'.

Between June 1783 and August 1787, Bligh plied the seas between the West Indies and England on Campbell's ships, carrying cargoes

Bligh, an engraving by J. Conde.

A later watercolour of the *Bounty* by Gregory Robinson.
Formerly the *Bethia*, she was a West Indies trader
brought from Duncan Campbell by the navy for
the expedition.

took place between Bligh and the master of the *Bounty,* John Fryer. It was over an administrative matter of the countersigning of the ship's books. Bligh signed. Fryer refused to sign unless Bligh signed a paper 'the purport of which was that he (Fryer) had been doing nothing amiss during his time on board'. Bligh summoned all hands and read the Articles of War and its penalties for disobedience—'this troublesome man saw his error and before the whole ship's company signed the books and here again I forgave him', wrote Bligh.

From this atmosphere of death, sickness and dissension, from the rigours of the long cold crossing, often against contrary winds, the monotonous diet and the inevitable frictions, the sudden projection into the breathless beauty of Tahiti was overwhelming.

The *Bounty* and crew was only the seventh European contingent to visit Tahiti since its formal discovery by Captain Wallis in the *Dolphin* on June 19, 1767. Knowing his dependence on the Polynesians for supplies and breadfruit Bligh was careful to tell the crew how to behave. They were not to speak of the way in which Captain Cook died, and were to conduct themselves with dignity. They were examined for venereal diseases as 'it could not be expected that the intercourse of my people with the native should be of a very reserved nature'. All were clean.

That Sunday, October 26, 1788, was the fateful day on which the *Bounty* crew were introduced to the wonders of Tahiti. The *Bounty* was so crowded with visitors that it was difficult to anchor in Matavai Bay so they anchored out where they were, moving closer

inshore the following morning. News and presents were exchanged and an abundance of island produce (pigs, bananas, coconut, some breadfruit) was received. While Bligh was busy establishing good relations with the district chiefs, the men were developing other friendships. Bligh, like Cook, tells us little of the sexual activities of his crew but Bligh wrote of their second day in port: 'at sunset all our male visitors left the ship'. By the following day Bligh recorded that 'an intimacy between the natives, and our people, was already so general that there was scarce a man in the ship who had not his tyo or friend'. This was to be the cause of some of Bligh's nastier moments while in Tahiti and no doubt was a prime motive for the mutiny. Bligh wanted to make contact with Otoo, the chief of the district of Matavai, a man well known to Cook and Bligh. Otoo was away at the time but he came quickly when he heard of Bligh's arrival.

Bligh sent Christian in a boat to bring Otoo on board where he learnt to his surprise that he was now known as Tinah, the name Otoo having been taken by his eldest son. Tinah brought his wife Iddeah and some of his family with him, and after presents were exchanged they dined on board—the men first, the women about an hour later. Tinah, as a major chief, was fed by an attendant, a custom he was most strict in—once when he dined on the

Stowage arrangements for breadfruit pots on the *Bounty.* The great cabin aft had to be sacrificed for the 'garden', leaving only small cabins for Bligh and the master and cramped quarters for the officers and crew. These conditions added to the usual hardships of an 18th century voyage.

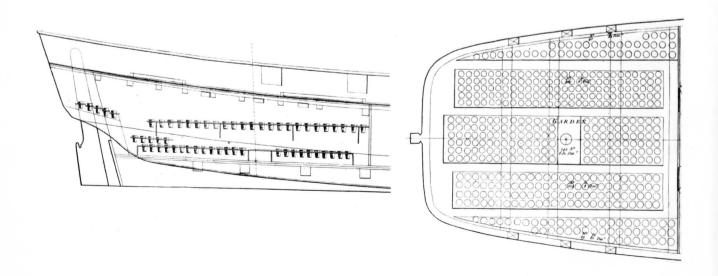

Bounty the attendants left early and Bligh himself had to lift the wine to his mouth. At this meeting Bligh gave him hatchets, adzes, files, gimlets, saws, mirrors, feathers and two shirts. Iddeah got ear-rings, necklaces and beads; but more sensibly asked Bligh for iron, which he gave her.

Bligh's writings contain detailed observations of the life and customs of the island. He was forever making visits to nearby chiefs, entertaining on board, exchanging presents, attending dances and recording the fascinating Tahitian society. He found out what had happened to the various plants and animals Cook had brought there. Learning that only one cow was left and that there was a bull in another district he went out of his way to buy the cow and installed her with the bull. He was appalled by the practice of child killing used to limit population and, with some diffidence, suggested that migration to Australia might be an alternative.

He arranged for supplies of breadfruit plants with Tinah and established a potting camp at Point Venus. On Thursday, November 5, work started and by Saturday they had collected 252 plants. But it emerged that midsummer was the wrong season for transplanting breadfruit, since many of these did not strike. Ultimately 302 plants were rejected and Bligh's long stay of five months in Tahiti was mainly because he had to ensure successful transplanting. This enforced delay was nearly disastrous for, as the days passed, new troubles beset them.

There were the usual thefts by the iron-hungry Tahitians and these irritated Bligh especially because he felt his crew's negligence was mainly to blame. Then it was discovered that four new sails were mildewed and rotten in many places, although Bligh had been assured they were in good order. 'Scarce any neglect of duty can equal the criminality of this', Bligh wrote. The alcoholic surgeon died and was buried ashore. The open roadstead of Matavai became dangerous in the more frequent westerlies. They moved to Toahroah Harbour, well protected by the reef but with so tricky an entrance that they ran aground and got off only after much difficulty. The most serious episode was the desertion, in the early hours of Monday, January 5, 1789, of Charles Churchill, master at arms, and two seamen, William Musprat and John Millward, in the small cutter with some guns. The mate of the watch, midshipman Thomas Hayward, was asleep at the time, and Bligh, riled by his incompetence, disrated Hayward and put him in irons for over a month. Bligh learned the deserters had taken a native canoe and headed for Ile Tetiaroa, a small atoll about 20 miles north of Tahiti. Seventeen days later they gave themselves up but only after Tinah's brother, Oreepyah, and another Tahitian had chased them to the island, at Bligh's request. They returned to Tahiti where Bligh arrested them. Churchill got 12 lashes and Musprat and Millward 24 each, and they were imprisoned. Three weeks later the punishment was repeated and these three were released.

This desperate bid for freedom had a further consequence not realized by Bligh. On Friday, February 6, they discovered that two strands of the three-stranded anchor cable had been cut, putting the *Bounty* in great peril. Another witch hunt ensued and it was Tinah who felt the first blast of Bligh's anger. Bligh considered it serious not only because of the threat presented to the safety of the ship, but because he feared that Tahitians were secretly plotting the *Bounty's* destruction. Bligh finally accepted Tinah's explanation that it was a member of an enemy tribe, perhaps, from Moorea, who had cut the rope. Rumours flourished among the crew, who doubted that a native would have the courage. A more convincing story was heard by the mutineers when they returned to Tahiti. Whydooah, Tinah's brother and a great warrior and drunkard, was a close friend of Hayward and was furious that Bligh had put him in irons. Indeed, he had decided to kill Bligh if he had flogged Hayward along with the deserters. He had cut the cable so that the ship would be driven on shore. He assumed the crew would then have to leave the ship and he would be able to free Hayward.

There were more troubles. Isaac Martin was flogged for striking a Tahitian and on March 2, a major robbery occurred on shore. The native culprit was caught by Tinah, given 100 lashes and imprisoned on board. A few days later he escaped and Bligh complained at the neglect of the officer of the watch, Mr Stewart, who was responsible for the prisoners. Bligh's verbal orders were being ignored and he now resorted to writing them out. Their stay was straining the resources of their hosts and on March 16, one district stopped the sale of pigs. Matavai and Oparre districts were also running low in supplies and, when the *Bounty* left, a moratorium was imposed in three districts to enable stocks to replenish.

They left on April 4, 1789, with 1,015 breadfruit plants and many other fruits.

Transplanting the breadfruit trees.

CHAPTER V

Mutiny

BOUNTY

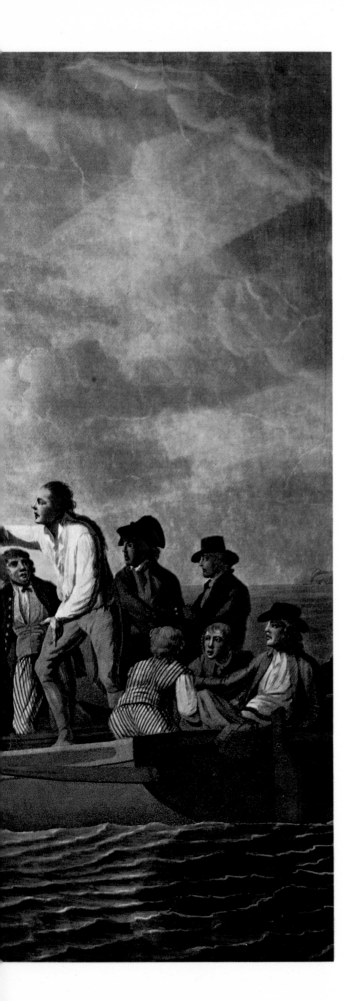

**Cutlasses being thrown to the launch before Bligh
is cast adrift by the mutineers. By R. Dodd.**

for this fortnight past', to have contemplated such a desperate escape. But Christian did not get a chance to go in the first and middle watches, and was then called to take over the morning watch. It was now, following hints from his earlier helpers, that he resolved to seize the ship. His watch had a number of the *Bounty's* most recalcitrant men, most of whom had been flogged at Bligh's command—Quintal, Martin, Churchill, Alexander Smith, John Williams, Muspratt and Millward. Pretending he wanted to shoot a shark, Christian was able to get the key to the arms chest and handed muskets to his friends.

Christian and the others surprised Bligh in his sleep. Under threat of a bayonet at his heart, he was hauled out of bed and his hands tied behind his back. Bligh yelled for help. Suddenly the ship was in turmoil. Bligh saw Fryer, the master, in the cabin opposite, but although he was the only uncommitted officer with pistols, Fryer made no move to help Bligh. Christian had posted guards over the officers' cabin and the forehatch, so no other help was possible. Bligh was taken to the stern where he was guarded by Christian and the armed mutineers.

'What is the cause of such a violent act?'

'I'll pawn my honour, I'll give my bond, Mr Christian, never to think of this if you desist'.

Bligh tried to dissuade Christian, reminding him of their family friendship, but Christian replied—

'No, Captain Bligh, if you had any honour, things had not come to this; and if you had any regard for your wife and family, you should have thought of them before and not behaved so much like a villain'. Again Bligh tried to speak, but, threatening him with a cutlass, Christian dismissed the entreaties—

'Hold your tongue, Sir, or you are dead this instant'.

With Bligh now guarded and isolated at the stern, Christian's plan emerged. The small cutter, a 'rotten carcase of a boat' was hoisted out, but others protested that this was a death-trap. So Christian ordered the launch to be used instead. The deck of the *Bounty* became a shambles as Christian summoned the loyalists into the launch. Some pleaded to stay with Christian, but were ordered off, while a few were told to stay on the *Bounty* against their wishes. The carpenter, Purcell, was put into the launch, Christian not wanting the company of that troublemaker, and when he took his tools into the launch, the mutineers said—

'Damn my eyes, he will have a vessel built within a month'. Mr Samuels, Bligh's clerk, bravely got some bread and Bligh's quadrant and compass into the launch; water, sailing gear and clothing were thrown aboard so that she sunk lower and lower, the mutineers 'laugh (ing) at the situation of the boat, being very deep and not room for those who were in her'. All were in the launch except Bligh.

Christian, Bligh wrote, was: 'plotting instant destruction on himself and everyone, for of all diabolical looking men, he exceeded every possible description'. Christian addressed Bligh: 'Come, Captain Bligh, your officers and men are now in the boat and you must go also; if you attempt to make the least resistance you will be instantly put to death'. Then Christian forced Bligh at bayonet point to the *Bounty's* side. Bligh said he appealed to Christian: 'was this a proper return for the many instances he had received of my friendship?' Bligh wrote: 'He appeared disturbed at my question and answered with much emotion, "That, Captain Bligh, is the thing; I am in hell, I am in hell".'

Bligh's hands were untied and he was forced into the launch. When Bligh asked for his Commission and sextant he was given them, with his pocket book and private journal. Four cutlasses and some pork were added but no firearms.

'After having undergone a great deal of ridicule, we were at last cast adrift in the open ocean'. It was only 8 a.m. As they commenced to row for Tofua, they heard a triumphant shout from the *Bounty,* 'Huzza for Otaheite'.

Those with Bligh in the launch were: John Fryer, master; Thos. Ledward, surgeon; David Nelson, botanist; William Peekover, gunner; William Cole, boatswain; William Purcell, carpenter; William Elphinston, master's mate; Thomas Hayward and John Hallet, midshipmen; John Norton and Peter Linkletter, quartermasters; Lawrence Lebogue, sailmaker; John Smith, Thomas Hall, Robert Tinkler and Robert Lamb, AB's; George Simpson, quartermaster's mate, and Mr Samuels, clerk.

Those with Christian in the *Bounty* were: George Stewart, acting master's mate; Peter Heywood and Edward Young, midshipmen; Charles Churchill, corporal; John Mills, gunner's mate; James Morrison, boatswain's mate; Thomas Burkitt, Mathew Quintal, John Sumner, John Millward, William McKoy, Henry Hillbrant, William Muspratt,

Alex Smith, John Williams, Thomas Ellison, Isaac Martin, Richard Skinner, Mathew Thompson, all AB's; William Brown, botanist's assistant.

Those kept on the *Bounty* against their will were Joseph Coleman, armourer; Charles Norman, carpenter's mate; Thomas McIntosh, carpenter's crew; and Byrne the fiddler.

Ship's chronometer used by Captain Bligh. He was scrupulous in checking the accuracy of his chronometers, which were a relatively new instrument of European navigation.

CHAPTER VI

3,000 miles in an open boat

Bligh's spirits rallied after being cast adrift: 'As soon as I had time to reflect, I felt an inward satisfaction which prevented any depression of my spirits. Conscious of my integrity, and with anxious solicitude for the good of the service in which I had been engaged, I found my mind wonderfully supported, and I began to conceive hopes, notwithstanding so heavy a calamity that I should one day be able to account to my King and country for the misfortune'.

His position was precarious, though he was most fortunate that Christian put them in the launch, for this was traditionally the longest and best rowing boat on the ships of those days. The curious bowed wood over the stern shown in the plan was a small derrick used to handle anchor cables. The thickened cross piece amidships was a windlass for heaving in. She had powerful and firm sections and it has been calculated that she weighed 5.57 tons all up with the mere seven inches of free board when she was first cast-off. She was 23 feet long, six feet nine inches wide and drew two feet nine inches of water, and with 19 men and gear was dangerously overloaded particularly as she was an open boat without decking.

Their stores were scanty—150 lb of bread, 32 lb of pork, six quarts of rum, six bottles of wine, 28 gallons of water and a few containers. They had four cutlasses but no firearms. Appraising his crew, Bligh realized that he had the weakest with him—the botanist, two cooks, a boy, the butcher, the clerk, quartermaster's mate, the gunner and the intractable carpenter. He had the sextant with some other navigational equipment, canvas, twine and tools.

It was calm on that afternoon of April 28, 1789. At about 4 p.m. an easterly reached them and they sailed to Tofua. They arrived in darkness and, the land in the lee being steep and rocky, they spent the night close under the shelter of the island with two men rowing to keep them in the one spot. Bligh planned to take on breadfruit and water at Tofua, then sail to Tongatabu, the largest island in the south of the Tongan group. He was familiar with the group because of the months he had spent around it with Cook. He would provision there for a trek to the East Indies, the nearest European settlement.

Next day they were to discover that Tofua was no tropical paradise. At 10 a.m. they found a rocky cove with a stony beach, hemmed in by cliffs. A party was sent ashore. They climbed the precipice by long vines put there by the Tongans but all they got was a little water. So they rowed further along the coast where they found coconut trees high on a cliff. They managed to get about 20 coconuts into the boat through the heavy surf and returned to the cove for another night, anchoring off the shore just clear of the surf.

It was in this cove that they narrowly escaped disaster. Dominated by the towering cliffs and fronting on dreary lava country containing little food or water, Tofua's active volcano glowed ominously in the distance. On returning from an expedition inland, Bligh was overcome with vertigo at the top of the cliff. He was helped down and reached the beach in a weak condition. That night Bligh and some of his crew stayed in a cave they discovered on the beach.

Bligh was determined not to use any of the bread or water in the boat and fed his party on meagre rations—an ounce of pork and two bananas for one meal, a boiled

68

banana for another. He persevered in exploration so that on Friday, May 1, they met a few Tongans. Trade started and a trickle of breadfruit, bananas, coconuts and water started to reach them. The weather was still bad and they stayed another day to get extra supplies. Bligh knew that if they failed to reach Tongatabu they would be forced to bear away to the westward, with no islands between them and the East Indies from which he could safely get food and water.

The native people increased in numbers the next day. Some arrived in canoes, and the stores mounted: 'everyone's spirits a little revived and they no longer regarded me with those anxious looks, which had constantly been directed towards me since we lost sight of the ship'. Their optimism was premature. Bligh was for a time deluded by the friendliness of the Tongans and was delighted to find amongst them an old acquaintance, Nageete, from Annamooka. When asked where his ship was, Bligh told them it had sunk. The situation changed as the Tongans realised the vulnerability of Bligh's party. More arrived and Bligh observed 'some symptoms of a design against us'. Some of the Tongans tried to haul the boat ashore and Bligh had to brandish his cutlass to make them stop. Now the staccato rhythm of stones being knocked together echoed around the cave and Bligh knew there would be trouble. This was the sign for an attack.

At noon Bligh gave some of the chiefs coconut and breadfruit with grand gestures of friendship. They asked him to sit down, but fearing this would give them a chance to grab him, he refused. There was nothing for it but to clear out as best they could. After dinner the crew, little by little, got the provisions into the boat—a difficult business because of the surf. The Tongans were lighting fires for the night and clearly planning an attack. The bulk of the stores were now in the boat and Bligh's journal, which he had been writing up in the cave, was retrieved despite an attempt by some Tongans to snatch it away.

What occurred next was a terrifying experience for Bligh and his crew.

It was nearly sunset when Bligh ordered the shore party aboard. Boldly they took their quota of things into the boat. Bligh was pressed to stay the night by the chiefs. Bligh replied 'no, I never sleep out of my boat; but in the morning we will again trade with you, and I shall remain until the weather is moderate, that we may go ... to Tongatabu'.

One chief then spoke, 'You will not sleep on shore? Then Mattie' (which directly signifies 'we will kill you'). The chiefs backed off, the knocking of the stones increased while Bligh, who chose to be accompanied by the carpenter at this point, took Nageete by the hand and 'we walked down the beach, every one in a silent kind of horror'.

Nageete asked Bligh to speak to one of the chiefs but Bligh realised this was a ruse and refused. Nageete moved away and Bligh made for the launch. He was getting aboard when John Norton, quartermaster, saw that the line holding the boat to the shore was still fast. Ignoring orders he leapt out of the boat and ran along the beach to free the rope.

The 200 Tongans attacked. Norton was stoned in an instant and some Tongans pulled on the stern line, nearly getting her ashore. A shower of stones rained on them, some 8lb in weight. Bligh cut the line. Norton's

Bligh and the launch crew hospitably received by the Governor at Timor, 1789. Watercolour by C. Benezach.

head was smashed with stones, and a brawl began over his trousers. Freed from the shore line the launch was dragged seawards by the bow anchor line but the anchor stuck. Luckily the fluke broke, oars were shipped, and they struggled to sea.

But the launch was not out of danger: 12 Tongans followed them in canoes. Again stones splashed around them, for the launch was slow and easily overtaken. Bligh threw some clothes overboard which the Tongans stopped to pick up: 'by this means with the night coming on they at last quitted us to reflect on our unhappy situation'.

Bligh realized he was now completely dependent on his own meagre resources. Used to the safety and power of a large armed ship, accustomed to supplies from respectful islanders, he was now isolated in the wilderness of the Pacific Ocean, in an overloaded and unarmed boat. It was too risky to rely on supplies from islands he might strike on the way to the East Indies, because the launch was all too vulnerable to attack. The men knew this too and asked Bligh to take them towards home; they agreed to live on one ounce of bread and a quarter of a pint of water a day. He had no map, but relying on memory he set a course for the Dutch settlement he had heard of at Timor, 3,618 miles away through the Fiji Islands. Of this challenge Bligh wrote 'I was happy, however, to see that everyone seemed better satisfied with our situation than myself'.

Sunday, May 3, 1789: The rough seas which had kept them at Tofua worsened during their first day out. The gale was so bad that the boat was becalmed between the rollers and when on top of the waves the wind hit the sail and she was almost overpowered. The sea curled over the stern. They bailed continually: 'a situation equally horrible perhaps was never experienced'. They dumped surplus clothes, sails and rope and stowed the bread, which had to be kept dry at all costs, in the carpenter's chest. The ultimate test came later that day when the wind increased and shifted, producing a confused and higher sea . . . 'and fatigue of bailing . . . was exceedingly great. We could do nothing more than keep before the sea; in the course of which the boat performed so well that I no longer dreaded any danger in that respect'.

The little ship had proved herself, at least. Now it remained for the men to survive, and the hardships they had to face began to alarm them. They were soaked and the night was so cold that their limbs were numbed and useless in the morning. A teaspoon of rum was served and this did some good. They sighted and passed safely through the Lau Group, which lies between Tonga and Fiji, making an incredible 95 mile noon to noon run. Despite the enormous difficulties Bligh persevered with his navigation, making a log line to check off the distance run. They lived on a few broken pieces of breadfruit for one meal, bits of yam for breakfast, and they prayed.

As the weather improved, they made good progress into the heart of the Fiji group. Now in the shelter of the land Bligh charted them and noted how mountainous and fruitful they looked. Although Tasman and Cook had touched on the group in their earlier voyages, Bligh's account was the most detailed to date and for some time they were known as Bligh's Islands. Between Viti Levu and Vanua Levu they passed over a coral reef with only four feet of water over it and with 'no russle of the sea to give us warning'. The shallow draft of the launch saved them, for a larger ship would have wrecked.

Cold, cramped and suffering from thirst, they sighted the Yasawa Group on Thursday, May 7, across what is now called Bligh Water. An unexpected current set them towards a rocky islet which they barely cleared by rowing. Two sailing canoes appeared, approaching swiftly, and the men rowed desperately to shake them off. After a nightmarish chase of some hours, the Fijians gave up as a storm, with thunder, lightning and torrential rain, enveloped them.

They collected 34 gallons of water and were able to relieve their thirst, only to pass the night sodden and shivering. The ration for Friday, May 8, was 1½ oz of pork, a teaspoonful of rum, ½ pint of coconut milk and 1 oz of bread. The weather improved.

Facing the long journey to Timor with few intervening islands, Bligh set about improving the boat. She was cleaned out and dried. Scales were made, from two coconut shells and a pistol ball, as a bread measure, and the rigging was strengthened. The stern was raised nine inches by nailing on some of the boat's seats, and a curtain of canvas was fixed round to give more shelter. Bligh instructed the men in the geography of Australia and New Guinea so that if he was lost they would be able to find their way to Timor 'which at present they knew nothing of, more than the name, and some not even that'.

The preparations were timely for a gale blew up on Saturday, May 9 evening and continued for three days. Wednesday was squally, and fresh gales hit them on Thursday, May 14, when they first sighted Vanua Lava, one of the Banks Islands in the New Hebrides. 'The sight of these islands served only to increase the misery of our situation. We were very little better than starving, with plenty in view, yet to attempt procuring any relief was attendant with so much danger... I consider the general run of cloudy and wet weather to be a blessing of Providence. Hot weather would have caused us to die with thirst.'

Storms, dark gloomy weather, pursued them. Navigation was uncertain. Bailing incessantly, always wet, the men pleaded for extra food which Bligh refused. The ardours of the journey wracked their bodies and Bligh resolved to make for Australia and then pass through Torres Strait to ensure a fair wind and perhaps food and rest. By Wednesday, May 20, still in wet, cold weather, Bligh described his crew: 'some of my people seemed half dead, our appearances were horrible, and I could look no way but I caught the eye of someone in distress. Extreme hunger was now too evident... the little sleep we got was in the midst of water and we constantly awoke with severe cramps and pains in our bones'.

The extract from Bligh's Narrative for Friday, May 22, read: 'Stormy gales from ESE to SSE, a high sea and dark, dismal night. Our situation this day was extremely calamitous. We were obliged to take the course of the sea, running right before it, and watching with the utmost care, as the least error in the helm would in a moment have been our destruction. At noon it blew very hard and the foam of the sea kept running over our stern and quarters. I, however, got propped up and made an observation of the latitude, in 14°17' S distance 130 miles'.

On Sunday, May 24, they enjoyed the warmth of the sun for the first time in 15 days. They stripped and dried their clothes and Bligh checked the stores. He calculated they had 29 days' supplies left, insufficient if there were any mishaps. So, with incredible strength of mind, he reduced the rations to allow for 43 days; explaining the position to his crew, 'they cheerfully agreed to my proposal'.

Morale improved with the arrival of many birds, which indicated that land was near.

On Monday, May 25, they caught a noddy by hand. It was about the size of a small pigeon and was divided into 18 portions and eaten, bones and all. A booby the size of a duck was caught, and the body with entrails, beak and feet, was divided and the blood given to the three men most distressed from hunger. The method of distribution was called 'who shall have this?' One person turns his back and calls out to another, who is pointing at a portion to be allocated, the name of the person who is to get it.

The finer weather brought new troubles, sunburn and heatstroke. But driftwood was passed on May 27, and that evening they sighted the surest sign of land: 'the clouds remained fixed in the West'. At one o'clock the next morning, they came upon the surf on the Great Barrier Reef.

They skirted the reef heading northwards and found themselves caught in a bay of reef by a wind shift to the east. 'Our situation was becoming unsafe... we could effect but little with the oars, having scarce strength to

The drama of the mutiny and the lure of Tahiti caught public imagination. This theatrical fantasy was staged only a few months after Bligh's return to London.

ROYALTY-THEATRE,
Well-Street, near Goodman's-Fields.

This prefent THURSDAY, May 6, 1790,
WILL BE PRESENTED
A NEW MUSICAL PIECE, called
TAR againſt PERFUME:
Or, The SAILOR PREFERRED.
Coxfwain, Mr. MATHEWS. William, Mr. BIRKETT. Old Slop, Mr. REES.
And Monfieur Le Friz, (the Perfumer,) Mr. WEWITZER.
Sufan, Mifs WILLIAMS.
A NEW DANCE, compofed by Mr. BOURKE, called
THE MERRY BLOCK-MAKERS.
By Monf. FERRERE, Mad. FOUZZI, Mad FERRERE, Mr. JEANI, Mr. BOURKE, &c.
A MUSICAL ENTERTAINMENT, called
A PILL FOR THE DOCTOR:
Or, The TRIPLE WEDDING.
Sailor, Mr. BIRKETT. Dr. Lotion, Mr. REES. Farmer, Mr. MATHEWS.
And Peftle, the Doctor's Man, Mr. WEWITZER.
Polly, Mifs WILLIAMS Dorothy, Mrs. SAUNDERS.
Lydia, Mifs E. WILLIAMS. And Goody, Mrs. BURNETT.
To conclude with a DANCE by the Characters.
A FAVOURITE SONG, by Mifs DANIEL.
The Whole to conclude with (the 4th Time) A FACT, TOLD IN ACTION, called
The PIRATES:
OR,
The Calamities of Capt. BLIGH.
Exhibiting a full Account of his Voyage, from his taking Leave at the Admiralty.
AND SHEWING,
The BOUNTY falling down the River THAMES.
The Captain's Reception at OTAHEITE, and exchanging the Britifh Manufactures
for the BREAD-FRUIT TREES. With an OTAHEITEAN DANCE.
The Attachment of the OTAHEITEAN WOMEN to, and then Diftrefs at parting from, the BRITISH SAILORS.
An exact Reprefentation of
The SEISURE of Capt. BLIGH, in the Cabin of the BOUNTY, by the Pirates.
With the affecting Scene of forcing the Captain and his faithful Followers into the Boat.
Their Diftrefs at Sea, and Repulfe by the Natives of One of the Friendly Iflands.
Their miraculous Arrival at the Cape of Good Hope, and their friendly Reception by
the Governor.
DANCES and CEREMONIES of the HOTTENTOTS
On their Departure. And their happy Arrival in England.
Rehearfed under the immediate Inftruction of a Perfon who was on-board the Bounty, Store-Ship.
. The Doors to be opened at Half paft Five and to begin at Half paft Six o'Clock precifely.
BOXES, 3s. 6d.—PIT, 2s. 6d—FIRST GALLERY, 1s. 6d—UPPER GALLERY, 1s.
Nothing under full Price will be taken nor any Money returned:
Places for the Boxes may be taken at the Stage-Door from Ten till Three o'Clock every Day.
VIVANT REX & REGINA.
☞ BOOKS of the PILL for the DOCTOR to be had at the Theatre; and, to prevent Impofition,
the Proprietors have ordered that no more fhall be taken for them than SIX-PENCE each.

pull them'. Bligh thought he might have to push the launch over the reef but an opening was sighted and they rushed through on the wind and current to the welcome calm.

They had entered the reef a little to the north of Providential Channel. They coasted northwards for a few miles until they found a safe landing on an island which Bligh called Restoration Island. Next day, May 29, their spirits much improved, they discovered water, collected oysters, heart of palm and edible berries. But the very improvement in the men brought its own troubles. Bligh found someone had got to the pork, which he could not keep locked. So he served the remaining 2 lb for dinner that night. He noticed discontent from some, 'even the master Fryer', at the smallness of the helpings and his difficulties grew with Fryer and the carpenter, Purcell. They sailed to another island (Sunday Island) to the northward where a more serious challenge to Bligh's authority developed. His commands were ignored culminating in an ultimatum from Purcell, who declared he was as good a man as Bligh—'I did not just now see where this was to end. I, therefore, determined to strike a final blow at it and either to preserve my command or die in the attempt, and taking hold of a cutlass, I ordered the rascal to take hold of another and defend himself. The master now instead of backing his commander and seizing the villain of a mutineer called out to the boatswain (William Cole) to put me in arrest...I was going to kill him but Mr Nelson now began to support my authority and I told the master that if he ever presumed to interfere while I was in the execution of my duty and that should any trouble in future arise, I would instantly put him to death the first person'. Fryer then promised Bligh his support in the future but Bligh recognised that both the master and the carpenter were dangerous. Because they were close to the mainland where he had seen Aborigines, Bligh left Sunday Island for a sandy key which lay further off-shore. Difficulties continued. Sunstroke and sickness from native berries afflicted some of the men. The master Fryer alarmed them all by insisting on his own fire which spread to the grass and blazed up fiercely. Bligh was afraid that this would signal their presence to the Aborigines so they left at dawn the next day, June 2.

After stopping at Turtle Island, the launch

A modern representation of Bligh and his crew set adrift from the Bounty.

carefully negotiated the northernmost point of Australia, with Bligh regretting that he did not have the time to check out the Strait further north. But he successfully traversed Torres Strait's dangerous, reef-strewn waters and reached the Arafura Sea on June 3, headed for Timor.

They made good progress but an alarming deterioration took place in the health of many of the crew despite an increase in the bread ration. Seas broke over the launch, rain soaked them, 'an extreme weakness, swelled legs, hollow and ghastly countenances, great propensity to sleep and an apparent debility of understanding, give me melancholy proofs of an approaching dissolution of my people, if I cannot get to land in a few days'. Luckily they caught a fish, the first in all those miles of sailing, and some birds. Then on Thursday, June 11, Bligh calculated they had passed the eastern point of Timor and the next day they sighted land, 'with an excess of joy'.

Bligh could not remember where the Dutch settlement was situated on Timor and so he skirted the southern coast, close-to, hoping to sight it. Fryer and Purcell pressed for an early landing but Bligh felt this was as dangerous in the isolated parts of Timor as in Fiji, and rejected the idea. Later that day they made contact with a coastal village, and, with a friendly East Indian as a pilot, rounded the western tip of Timor and made their way to Coupang. They arrived on Sunday, June 14, 1789.

Thus ended one of the greatest feats of European seamanship. Bligh can be excused for self congratulation when he wrote 'indeed it is scarce within the scope of belief that in 41 days I could be on the coast of Timor, in which time we have run by our log 3,618 miles which on average is 90 miles a day... notwithstanding our extreme distress no one should have perished on the voyage'. Resting in Coupang, Bligh reflected that the 'provisions with which we left the ship was no more than we should have consumed in five days...the mutineers must naturally have concluded that we could have no other place of refuge than the Friendly Islands'.

His party was given every assistance in Timor. After recuperation (although poor Nelson the botanist died there) Bligh bought a 34-foot schooner which he named HMS *Resource,* and towing the launch she reached Batavia, via Samarang, on October 1, 1789. Bligh was at all times zealous in the care of his crew but the humid and unhealthy climate of Batavia was too much for some of the survivors. Thomas Hall, cook, died, and after Bligh left for England by a Dutch boat, two more were buried. En route for England, as passages became available, Lamb died and Ledward was never heard of again. Of the 19 who left the *Bounty* in the launch, only 12 lived to return to England.

Reading Bligh's account, the overriding impression of the man is of his tremendous will power, intelligence and energy. He coped with the dangers of the sea, starvation rations, the fractious members of his crew, navigation with inadequate equipment and yet had time to draw charts and make most detailed comments on the lands and peoples he observed. His average progress of 90 miles a day would do credit to a modern yacht of similar size.

A fair sample of English reaction to the voyage is the comment of William Windham, Pitt's spokesman in the Commons: 'But what officers you are, you men of Captain Cook; you rise upon us in every trial!'

Bligh was re-united with his wife and his 'little angels'. Mrs Bligh had been pregnant when he left, and he had written from Timor sending his blessing to 'my dear little stranger'—which turned out to be twin daughters, Frances and Jane.

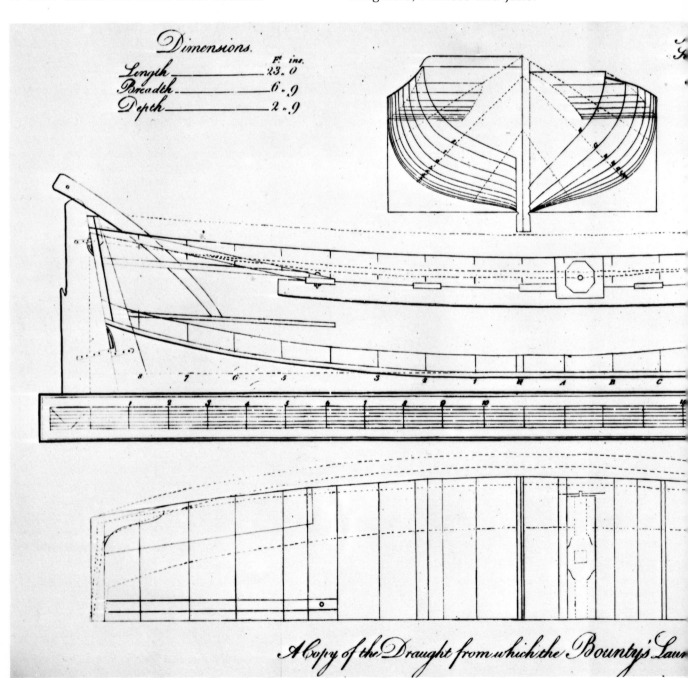

Dimensions.

	F.t. ins.
Length	23. 0
Breadth	6 . 9
Depth	2 . 9

A Copy of the Draught from which the Bounty's Laun

Within a few days, the influential Heywood family wrote to him asking for news of young Peter. Bligh, convinced that the boy had actively supported Christian, replied: 'His ingratitude to me is of the blackest dye, for I was a father to him in every respect, and he never once had an angry word from me through the whole course of the voyage, as his conduct always gave me much pleasure and satisfaction. I very much regret that so much baseness formed the character of a young man I had a real regard for, and it will give me much pleasure to hear that his friends can bear the loss of him without much concern'. Peter Heywood's family, particularly his devoted sister Nessy, were not convinced of his 'baseness', however, and continued to pray for his safe return.

The story of the mutiny and the launch voyage was a sensation in London. Within two months the Royalty Theatre advertised 'A Fact, Told in Action, called The Pirates: or, The Calamities of Capt. Bligh', including 'The attachment of the Otaheitean Women to, and then Distress at parting from, the British Sailors'. The latter aspect of the affair caught the imagination of the public more than anything else. In Bligh's own 'Narrative of the Mutiny on Board His Majesty's Ship *Bounty*; and the Subsequent Voyage...', published at the end of that year, he asserted that the mutiny was the result of the corruption and demoralization of his men due to the delightful women of Tahiti and the life of ease they led there. Indeed, even for the relatively privileged Young Gentlemen on board, Tahiti must have seemed like Paradise; especially after the rigours of that voyage with their crusty commander.

A six-penny account of the mutiny was soon for sale on the streets of London, offering a curious public: 'Secret Anecdotes of the Otaheitian Females'. After describing ceremonial performances of 'the rites of Venus', the author mused on 'whether the scheme attending certain actions which are allowed on all sides to be in themselves innocent, is implanted in nature, or superinduced by custom?' All the same, the amorous mutineers were stigmatized as villains and pirates, especially Christian.

The Admiralty immediately made plans to pursue the mutineers, and acquitted Bligh for the loss of the *Bounty* at a brief court martial. Bligh had his revenge on Purcell, who was charged with disobedience and contempt, and reprimanded. (Later, it appears, Purcell went insane.) However, Bligh took no action against Fryer.

Bligh was most gratified to be presented to King George III at Court, and he was also promoted to Commander of the sloop *Falcon*. Then, on December 15, 1790, as a special mark of favour, the all-important promotion to post captain was announced, setting him safely on the ladder of advancement by seniority.

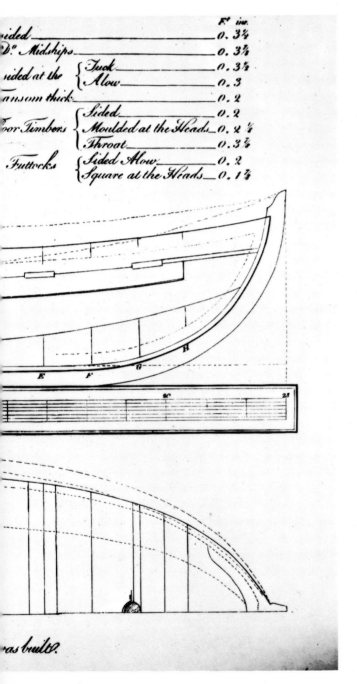

The lines of the *Bounty's* open launch in which Bligh and 18 crew travelled 3,618 miles from Tofua to Timor. They were fortunate to be put in the launch instead of the *Bounty's* worm-eaten cutter.

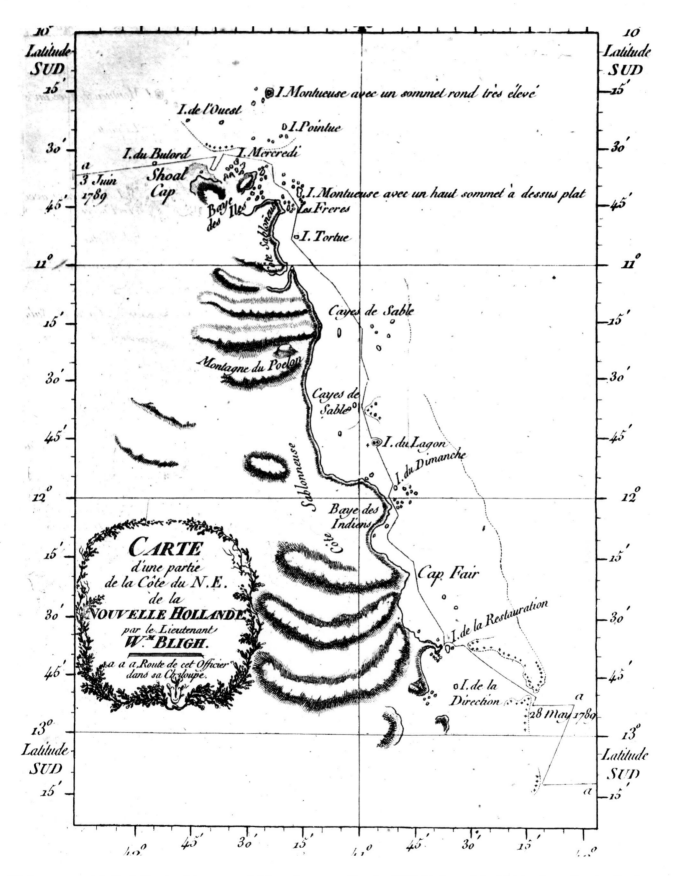

Bligh, now a celebrity following his successful launch
voyage, was painted in London, 1790, by J. Russell.

Track of Bligh's launch inside the Great Barrier Reef,
Australia, published in a French translation of Bligh's
Narrative of the mutiny and the launch voyage. Both
were published in 1790.

CHAPTER VII

Mutineers

A
VOYAGE
TO THE
SOUTH SEA,
UNDERTAKEN BY COMMAND OF
HIS MAJESTY,
FOR THE PURPOSE OF
CONVEYING THE BREAD-FRUIT TREE
TO THE WEST INDIES,
IN HIS MAJESTY's SHIP THE BOUNTY,
COMMANDED BY
LIEUTENANT *WILLIAM BLIGH.*

INCLUDING AN ACCOUNT OF THE
MUTINY ON BOARD THE SAID SHIP,
AND THE
SUBSEQUENT VOYAGE of Part of the CREW, in the SHIP's BOAT,
From TOFOA, one of the FRIENDLY ISLANDS,
To TIMOR, a DUTCH SETTLEMENT in the East Indies.

THE WHOLE ILLUSTRATED WITH CHARTS, &c.

PUBLISHED BY PERMISSION OF THE
LORDS COMMISSIONERS OF THE ADMIRALTY.

LONDON:
PRINTED FOR GEORGE NICOL, BOOKSELLER TO HIS MAJESTY, PALL-MALL.

M.DCC.XCII.

With Bligh gone, Christian dumped the breadfruit overboard, and headed the *Bounty* for Tubuai in the Austral Group, 330 miles south of Tahiti. Few ships visited the island, and it would have been an ideal spot for the mutineers were the Tubuaians not so hostile. After a first encounter in which 12 Tubuaians were killed, Christian sailed back to Tahiti. Although royally received, Christian still feared discovery and decided it would be safer to try once more to force his presence on the Tubuaians.

With provisions, livestock and 28 Tahitians, the *Bounty* went back to Tubuai, where work was begun on building a permanent settlement. Christian's troubles started with his own people, who were lazy and generally uncooperative. Having thrown off Bligh's authority they were not pleased to accept Christian's. When the Tubuaians began a series of attacks on the intruders, Christian decided they had better leave. They sailed back to Tahiti. There the party split up, eight remaining with Christian on the *Bounty,* the rest going ashore with provisions and guns.

The *Bounty* had about 28 aboard; nine white men, now with wives, and six Tahitian men, of whom three had wives. Influenced by his reading of a book by Captain Phillip Carteret, Christian decided on Pitcairn Island as their destination.

By January, 1790 they were well established on shore. They burnt the *Bounty;* it might be seen by a passing ship and also, of course, it was quite damning to them as evidence.

They lived in apparent peace for two years. Then one of the white men, Williams, lost his wife; she was killed when she fell over a cliff. Williams immediately demanded the wife of one of the Tahitians. This Tahitian was then killed by several other Tahitians at the instigation of Christian.

Some time elapsed before the next of what was to be a series of violent deaths. The Tahitians shot and killed five of the *Bounty* men, including Christian, apparently having had enough of the white man's arrogance. Then the womenfolk murdered all the Tahitian men, leaving only four *Bounty* men. Of these McCoy fell off a cliff whilst drunk and the bully Quintal was murdered by Young and Adams on Christmas Day, 1800.

Young and Adams did their best to restore the moral tone of the community, instituting

regular prayer meetings. Young died naturally and John Adams, otherwise known as Alexander Smith, survived to tell his story to the outside world.

Adams was discovered in 1808 when Captain Folger, commanding an American Whaler, called at Pitcairn and was very much surprised to find this community of English-speaking people.

Six years later two British warships also came upon the community and sent a report to the Admiralty.

In 1856 the 194 inhabitants were relocated on Norfolk Island, as over-population threatened Pitcairn's self-sufficiency. Some later returned to Pitcairn, but many of the descendants of the original community remained on Norfolk Island.

Meanwhile, of the 16 who chose to remain on Tahiti, there were true mutineers, half-hearted mutineers and others who had simply been refused permission to accompany Bligh. Some of them were to suffer and others to die in as ugly a way as Christian's party. But that was well in the future.

The first months on Tahiti they lived in a state of tension wondering what the authorities might do to them when they were eventually and inevitably picked up. Would the innocent be able to prove their innocence? Would there be any pardons for the half-hearted?

Most were determined to surrender voluntarily, calculating that this would make a favourable impression at the inevitable trial. With determination and skill, ten of them, led by Morrison, spent nearly eight months building a 30 foot boat (named *Resolution*) with the hope of sailing to Batavia, and then to England. But they could not equip her adequately, and the plan was given up. In another part of the island two of the active mutineers, Churchill and Thompson, were murdered; Thompson appears to have lost his temper and, after indiscriminately killing two Tahitians, he killed Churchill. Whereupon the Tahitians tricked Thompson into believing they remained friendly and, when he drew near, smashed his skull with a stone.

In March 1791 seven took the *Resolution* on a jaunt to the south coast of the main island; on March 23, the outside world caught up with them with the arrival of HMS *Pandora* under Captain Edward Edwards. Eighteen months of tropical freedom was ended and they were to embark on a journey almost as remarkable as Bligh's.

The Admiralty had moved quickly on

receiving Bligh's account of the mutiny and the *Pandora,* a 24 gun frigate, was sent to find them. Besides rounding up the mutineers Edwards was instructed to survey Endeavour (Torres) Strait. Bligh commented, 'Capt. Edwards will never return as he did not know the navigation of Endeavour Straits'.

With some difficulty Edwards rounded up the 14 remaining mutineers and indiscriminately herded them together in 'Pandora's Box', a small round deckhouse he had built in the stern. The only entrance was a 20 inch hole at the top and all wore hand cuffs or leg irons. 'The Box' stank. Maggots multiplied. Compounding their physical discomfort was the agonizing sight, for some, of their distressed Polynesian wives and children, repeatedly visiting the ship and pleading for their release.

The *Pandora* left Tahiti in May and looked for Christian and the other mutineers on Aitutaki Island and Palmerston Island, Cook Group. They tried the Tokelau Group, Samoa, Tofua and Wallis and then made for Torres Strait. Bligh's prediction was fulfilled, for Edwards continued sailing at night despite a warning from the lead line that the sea was shallowing. The *Pandora* struck on the night of August 28, 1791. Panic overcame the ship's company as the water rose. Edwards let McIntosh, Coleman and Norman (all loyalists) out of the Box to help with the pumps, but he behaved with the utmost cruelty towards those remaining. Desperate to escape certain drowning, they had managed to break their irons—but Edwards ordered them to be renewed. At daybreak they pleaded with Edwards again and he released three; one of them was Byrne, the blind fiddler. There his compassion ended for Edwards fled overboard as the boat settled, but one of the *Pandora's* crew opened the lid of their prison. Six managed to escape but four drowned, still manacled in the Box.

Edwards was never confronted with his inhuman behaviour. The subsequent court martial on the shipwreck was formal, recording only that 'four of the mutineers were lost with the ship'.

Fortunately the *Pandora's* crew had been able to make reasonable preparations for getting to Timor by boat. After 19 days on a nearby sandy key, they set out in four boats. Edwards was now apparently mentally unbalanced. His treatment of the mutineers became obsessively vindictive. They were starved, tied to the boat's floor and given no shade from the sun. They lost their skin from

Dangerous Bounty Bay on Pitcairn Island. The lack of a safe anchorage and Captain P. Carteret's error in positioning Pitcairn isolated the mutineers for almost 20 years.

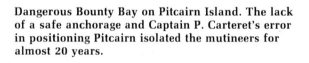

One of *Bounty's* massive anchors now at the Auckland Museum. The inscription in part reads: 'This historic anchor, intimately associated with the ill-fated HMS *Bounty*, is believed to have been abandoned by Fletcher Christian and his fellow mutineers in 1789, when they used it as a kedge to free the vessel from a coral shoal in the Papaea Arm of Matavai Bay, Tahiti.'

John Adams' house, Pitcairn.

Thursday October Christian, Fletcher Christian's son, born on Pitcairn Island. His Tahitian mother had taken the name of Isabella. Thursday later married the widow of Edward Young, one of the mutineers.

Another view of Point Venus, Tahiti, by Tobin. This is from seaward of the *Providence* and the *Assistant.*

Besides the tricky navigation, Bligh had to cope with attacks by Torres Strait Islanders. This watercolour by Tobin shows the *Providence* and the *Assistant* firing at the canoes, September 1792. One of the *Assistant's* crew died from an arrow wound.

Carrying the breadfruit safely through Torres Strait, the contingent called at Coupang, Timor, Bligh's refuge in the launch voyage. This view by George Tobin, 1792.

An Animal shot at Adventure Bay. It had a Beak like a Duck – a thick brown coat of Hair, through which the points of numerous Quills of an Inch long projected & were very sharp. – It was 17 Inches long & walked about 2 Ins from the Ground, had very small Eyes & five Claws on each foot. There was a small opening at the end of the Bill & had a very small tongue. – NB

One of Bligh's more interesting drawings—a parrot of Van Diemen's Land.

Bird of Van Diemen's Land, Bligh.

View of the *Providence* and the *Assistant* in Matavai Bay, by Tobin.

A heron of Van Diemen's Land drawn by Bligh.

Drawing and description by Bligh of a strange animal shot in Adventure Bay. It was not a platypus, as at first thought, but an echidna or native porcupine.

New Hebrides on August 30, 1792 he sighted the New Guinean coast.

Torres Strait lay before them. Bligh did not know that his prediction of the *Pandora's* shipwreck had come true, but, alive to the dangers, he sent the shallow-draft *Assistant* ahead to feel the way. As they entered the maze of reefs through a break called 'Bligh's Entrance', to the north of Cook's passage in the *Endeavour,* he posted a cutter and a whaleboat to lead the *Assistant.* It took them 19 days to negotiate the Strait. Great care had to be exercised. Captain Portlock wrote: 'from the masthead, with a good lookout, you may see and avoid danger from the colour of the water. The bottom can be seen in six or seven fathoms of water, many more I am confident. But people must not depend too much on this, for from six or seven fathoms you step on the reef, where there is not above two feet'. Fortunately the weather was fine and the water smooth. A brief encounter with the people of Torres Strait, when the small craft were separated from the main ships, was followed by a more serious episode a week later.

They were more than half-way through the Strait when about eight canoes, carrying some 100 warriors, came from an island near Warrior and Dungeness Islands. They gathered around both ships. Suddenly one canoe launched an attack with bows and arrows on the *Assistant* and her cutter, which was alongside. Fire was immediately returned and a signal made to the *Providence* for help. She was also attacked and besides using small arms, the *Providence* retaliated with a four-pounder. The raid was abortive, but three men on the *Assistant* were injured by arrows, one of whom died two weeks later.

Progress became extremely difficult as they felt their way out of the Strait. Both ships were caught in a nasty situation just north of Mulgrave Island when the tide carried them at a great rate through a narrow passage with shoal water. The anchor cable jammed on the *Providence* and it needed quick work in releasing the second anchor to prevent her crashing into the rocks. Safely anchored they found themselves surrounded by rocky reefs with the prospect of an even worse passage to the westward. The smallest depth, according to Flinders, was four fathoms. They got through. Flinders summed up the achievement: 'Thus was accomplished, in 19 days, the passage from the Pacific, or Great Ocean, to the Indian Sea; without other misfortune than what arose from the attack of the natives and some damage done to the cables and anchors. Perhaps no space of 3½ degrees in length, presents more dangers than Torres Strait, but with caution and perserverance, the Captains Bligh and Portlock proved them to be surmountable'.

Clear of the Strait they made good time to Coupang, Timor, where they were able to replenish their almost exhausted water supply. About 224 breadfruit had died from lack of water although they were given high priority on the voyage. Flinder's Journal notes that the thirsty men used to lick the drops of water that fell from the pots. From Timor they went via the Cape of Good Hope to St Helena and on January 23, 1793 they arrived at Kingstown Harbour, St Vincent. One load was put ashore there and on February 5 they anchored at Port Royal, Jamaica where the remaining breadfruit and other specimens were landed.

Jamaica subsequently honoured Bligh and Portlock with a gift of 1,000 and 500 guineas respectively but Bligh, always concerned over his professional status, was unable to accept the terms in which Portlock's gift was made. The Jamaican House of Assembly vote of thanks (22/11/1793) to Portlock read: 'For his important services in guiding the ship *Providence* through a very difficult and intricate navigation, whereby that ship was enabled to fulfill the end of her voyage, in introducing the breadfruit to this island'. Evidently someone set them straight. In December, 1794 they retracted that specific tribute, saying that the House 'meant to convey no other sense of his conduct than that he had acquitted himself of his duty in a manner much to his credit, while under the immediate directions of his commanding officer Captain Bligh, from whose merit they did not intend to detract'. This was sent to Bligh who wrote in 1795 thanking the House for the 1,000 guineas gift and 'for your vote in explaining the one to Lieutenant Portlock'.

While at Jamaica they learned that France had declared war on England. So the *Providence* was armed and stood by to defend Port Royal until reinforcements arrived. It was not until June 15 that they left and reached England in August, 1793 without difficulty.

There is no doubt in considering this voyage, that if the *Bounty* expedition had been mounted with the same thoroughness and cost, it would have succeeded. Perhaps Bligh behaved with more circumspection on this

The *Providence* and the *Assistant* in Adventure Bay,
Van Diemen's Land, 1792: Tobin. Bligh had been in the
bay twice before, once with Cook, then with the
Bounty.

Island of Maitea, or Mehetia, by George Tobin. Sixty
miles east of Tahiti, this was the last island sighted
before the *Providence* and the *Assistant* arrived
at Tahiti, April 1792.

second attempt, but he had marines to support him and more competent officers and crew.

Sir Joseph Banks certainly gained in reputation with his breadfruit transplantation, but his successful scheme for acclimatization in India of the tea plant from China was vastly more significant in its economic impact. The breadfruit did not become a staple in the West Indies. More important, the sugar industry of such colonies as Jamaica and St Vincent was approaching a crisis as Cuba and others emerged as cheap producers, and Napoleon started the production of beet sugar in Europe. Between 1799 and 1807, 65 plantations in Jamaica were abandoned, and many went bankrupt.

The *Providence* and the *Assistant* were paid off without any recrimination or ill-feeling amongst the crew. Bligh, according to a newspaper account at the time, 'was cheered on quitting the ship to attend the Commissioner; and at the dock-gates the men drew up and repeated the parting acclamation'.

The gold medal awarded to Bligh, 1794, by The Royal Society of Arts for his success in conveying the breadfruit to the West Indies.

But all was not well for the officers. Bligh had returned to meet the reaction in popular and official favour following the court martial of the *Bounty* mutineers. Tobin wrote 'that the popularity which attended the equipment of the expedition was considerably diminished towards its completion... it was not difficult to discover on our arrival that impressions had been received by many in the service, by no means favourable to him (Bligh). It is hard to believe that this could have extended to the officers of the *succeeding* voyage—yet we certainly thought ourselves rather in the background'.

Bligh was generous in his recommendations of his officers to the Admiralty. But he was treated rather distantly. Lord Chatham, First Sea Lord, and brother of William Pitt, Prime Minister, preferred to see Portlock, although Bligh waited on him daily. The Royal Society of Arts did however award Bligh the gold medal promised on the successful completion of the mission.

Native hut of Adventure Bay, Van Diemen's Land. George Tobin.

Port Praya, Island of St Jago, the second port of call of the *Providence* and the *Assistant* on the outward voyage, September, 1791: George Tobin. Bligh suffered from fever on this passage and was grateful for the consideration shown by his crew.

CHAPTER IX

Bligh
collects evidence

When Bligh left on the *Providence,* his description of the mutiny as one of the 'most atrocious acts of Piracy ever committed' was entirely accepted, and it was most unfortunate for Bligh that he was not in England to defend his reputation when the mutineers returned for trial. The life of Heywood and the honour of the Christian family were at stake and no efforts were spared to present Bligh in the worst possible light. The fickle public was captivated by the loyalty and distress of Heywood's sister, Nessy, and certainly it seemed a terrible thing for so young a lad to be put to death. The Christian interest was ably advanced by Fletcher's brother, Edward, who was a barrister. After the trial was over, he published the minutes of the proceedings, together with an appendix containing 'A full account of the real causes and circumstances of that unhappy Transaction, the most material of which have been hitherto withheld from the Public'.

This document was heralded in 'The Cumberland Pacquet' (Cumberland being the Christians' home county) as a commentary which would cause the public to correct 'the erroneous opinions, which, from certain false narratives, they have long entertained; and will be enabled to distinguish between the audacious and hardened depravity of the heart which no suffering can transform, and the desperation of an ingenuous mind, torn and agonized by unprovoked and incessant abuse and disgrace'.

Edward Christian had interviewed those from the *Bounty* crew who were in the country, and maintained that all declared that the ship's company had been greatly discontented at their short allowance of provisions. He denied that Christian had 'a favourite woman' in Tahiti, and said that Christian had been deeply depressed at Bligh's treatment of him. The men told him that, before the mutiny, Christian 'was generally below, leaning his head upon his hand, and when they came down for orders, he seldom raised his head to answer more than Yes or No'.

The document cited some instances of Bligh's cruelty to Christian, though these hardly seem sufficient reason for mutiny: Christian had command of the tent at Otaheite where Bligh entertained the chiefs sometimes, and before all the company used to abuse Christian for 'some pretended fault or other'. Also, Christian was 'taller than Bligh and a favourite with the Islanders'. He had taken the name of a chief in exchange for his own,

but Bligh injured his feelings by telling the chief that Christian was only his 'towtow' or servant.

Bligh found that altogether, he had much to answer for on his return. Some of his old crew provided affidavits in reference to Christian. Joseph Coleman, the armourer who had been kept on the *Bounty* against his will, swore: 'I remember Christian having a girl, and of her going with him to the island Tooboy (Tubaia), and lived with him'. John Smith, AB, who had been cast adrift with Bligh, swore: 'When in working the ship, and things had been neglected...I have known the Captain to be angry and damn the people, as is common; but the Captain immediately afterwards always behaved to the people as if nothing had happened'. Lawrence Lebogue, the sailmaker, who had also survived the launch voyage, added: 'I knew Captain Bligh was a very great friend to Christian the mutineer; he was always permitted to use the Captain's cabin, where I have seen the Captain teaching him navigation and drawing. He was permitted to use the Captain's liquor when he wanted it, and I have many times gone down at night to get him grog out of the Captain's case'. Lebogue also said that Bligh's anger 'never lasted the next minute' and that he remembered 'Christian had a girl, who was always with him'.

Unfortunately for Bligh, his published Narrative had excluded a great many details of the difficulties he faced with the officers and men. During their Tahitian idyll they had become quite disinterested in the ship and her system of discipline, even to the point of neglecting or disobeying orders. They became progressively involved in Tahitian society, marrying the women according to local custom, making them pregnant, and undergoing rituals of brotherhood with some of the Tahitian men. Bligh must indeed have seemed to them like an unpleasant bogeyman; a constant reminder of their responsibilities, their past, and the dreary future ahead of them once they quit the island. Bligh no doubt watched their alienation with disgust and perhaps a little jealousy. The sight of Christian, disporting

A view of the House of Commons on the late 18th century. It was a centre of privilege and patronage rather than a place of reform. Fox warned a half empty house that unless the reasons for the Spithead mutiny of 1797 were examined, others would break out. Within weeks the paralysing Nore mutiny erupted, involving Bligh and his ship, the *Director.* Eng. by B. Cole, 1772.

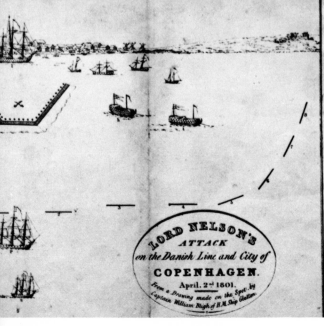

by his six growing daughters. His daughter Harriet married a Henry Aston Barker from Gloucester, and their first child, christened William Bligh Barker, arrived at the end of the year. (Some years later, Mrs Bligh wrote to her husband: 'This little Will Bligh is a darling fellow, I think equal to the first'.)

In March, 1803, he wrote to the Admiralty asking for another command. For the rest of the year he was employed in surveying, but in May, 1804, he was given the *Warrior*, an even finer ship than the *Irresistible*. War had broken out again. Nelson was leaving to blockade the Mediterranean, while Cornwallis and the Western Squadron guarded the western approaches to the English Channel, for Napoleon was looking for an opportunity to convey his Grand Army to Kent or to Ireland. The *Warrior* was to stay in home waters, part of the fighting force ceaselessly cruising off Ushant, guarding the Channel and blockading French ships in Brest harbour and further down the coast at Rochefort. First, the *Warrior* had to undergo repairs and painting at Plymouth Dock. In July, Bligh wrote to his wife telling her of his dinner ashore in 'a very good country house' with a friend of hers: 'She entertained me, for I have not laughed before since I left home, about Mrs Petree showing the lions, about Tonkins & his wife who, she says, is a little tygress, & of your amusement when you retired to your room in noticing the different characters you had dined with. She . . . showed me the artificial rose which Mary gave her, that she kept it in remembrance of you—it was in a handsome china jar on the chimney piece, in short, poor woman, she was fond of speaking of you, & I was very desirous to hear it in preference to any other conversation . . .'.

The *Warrior* left on her tour of duty in July and did not return until next November. It seems that, with the exception of his first-lieutenant, Johnston, Bligh faced the same kind of hostile confrontation as he had experienced on the *Monarch*. The trouble came to a head when Bligh arrested Lieutenant Frazier, whom he suspected of malingering, for refusing to keep his watch. Frazier had a swollen ankle which he claimed was too painful to allow him to come on deck—even with permission to

The British fleet under Nelson passing through the Sound towards Copenhagen.

Nelson's attack on the Danish line and City of Copenhagen, from a drawing made on the spot by Bligh who was in command of the *Glatton*. After the battle Nelson personally thanked Bligh for the brave conduct of the *Glatton*.

Medal awarded to William Bligh Esquire, The Dutch Fleet Defeated, Captain of HMS *The Director* on the 11 October, 1797.

remain seated during his watch. Bligh seems to have over-reacted in requiring Frazier to be court martialled for disobedience. Frazier was acquitted in November, and then, no doubt encouraged by Bligh's unpopularity, had Bligh court martialled for abusive language to him on that occasion, and for generally insulting, bullying and tyrannizing his crew, particularly the warrant and petty officers. Bligh's trial took place on the 25th and 26th of February, 1805. After hearing the evidence, the Court decided 'that the charges were in part proved, and did therefore adjudge Captain William Bligh . . . to be in future more correct in his language'. He was immediately returned to the command of his ship.

Except to the participants, this was an insignificant affair. Over-crowding, lack of privacy, and uncomfortable conditions led to perpetual surliness and quarrelling on all ships of the fleet, and courts martial aboard HM ships never ceased. If Bligh had not charged Frazier, he would not have been counter-charged himself. But the evidence given at the trial is another insight into Bligh's character and his relations with his men.

The only men who had not a good word to say about their captain were the four lieutenants, though even one of these admitted that he had never heard Bligh behave in a 'tyrannical, unofficerlike, or oppressive manner to any of his officers'. Lieutenant Boyack claimed that he had heard Bligh say 'he would

rule the officers of the *Warrior* with an iron rod' at the beginning of the voyage, but it appeared that Bligh already had evidence of their hostility at that time. Boyack also said that 'Captain Bligh's expressions to the officers before the ship's company lessed their dignity as officers and was degrading in the extreme'. There was a further clue to the lieutenants' umbrage when another witness suggested that Bligh used exactly the same sort of language to officers and men alike.

Many of the other witnesses called by Frazier prejudiced his case. John Amplet, a marine, said that Bligh had never been tyrannical or oppressive, though he had seen the captain come out of his cabin in a passion on finding the ship out of her station. Amplet said that both Frazier and Bligh had questioned him about his position prior to the trial, and added that Frazier had told him that he would be respected by every officer on the ship for speaking against Bligh. The master's mate asserted that Bligh had abused Frazier and shaken his fist in his face, but he had not heard Bligh abuse any of his officers before this, and he admitted that he had commented to various people on the *Warrior* that he had never sailed with a better captain in his life.

John Honeybone, a seaman, denied having heard Bligh call the master 'a dastardly old man and a Jesuit', though he had heard him tell Frazier that he 'was like the rest of his countrymen'. He said that on one occasion, when Captain Bligh was observing the sun with a sextant, Frazier gave him 'a jostle when he passed him'.

Samuel Jewell, boatswain, said that he had frequently been called 'you ——, you scoundrel and you villain' by Bligh, but he put no particular interpretation on the words, for the captain was very hot and hasty, and the words no sooner escaped him than his passion ended. On one occasion, Bligh had caught hold of him by the breast, shaken him, torn his shirt and called him 'a damned rascal' but—he added later—he would just as soon sail with Captain Bligh as with any other captain he knew.

All the witnesses for the prosecution agreed that Bligh used abusive language at some time or other, though few of them seemed disturbed by the fact. Most of them baulked at saying that he had generally been a bully and a tyrant.

Bligh called six witnesses in his defence. His first lieutenant, Johnston, said that he had been with Bligh for nearly three years on the *Director,* and then on the *Warrior,* and had never had occasion to complain of the captain's conduct towards him. He said that Bligh's general manner of giving directions was 'frequently swearing at the quarter masters or men of that description who were standing round, with a considerable motion of the hand, which was not only used on persons of that description, but generally in giving orders'. (Boyack had said that the captain often employed 'a great deal of action with his hands, as if he was going to knock any person down'.) Johnston also said, quite significantly, that he understood that the seamen 'had a high opinion of Captain Bligh's humanity and good conduct towards them'.

Peter Mills, a midshipman, claimed that Frazier had attempted to blackmail him into appearing on his side, saying that 'he would expose me to the Court, and produced a play-bill, in which my name was unfortunately placed. I told him that he might if he pleased, that while my Captain acted to me as a good officer, I would support him'. The rest of his evidence was rather spoiled by his admission that he had previously read a number of questions put to him by Bligh at the trial. Bligh later promoted Mills' career, though whether this was out of simple gratitude or whether this had been promised before the trial remains, of course, a matter for speculation. Mills claimed that he volunteered as a witness.

Mr Joseph Strephon, clerk of the *Warrior,*
denied that Bligh used improper language at all, though he had heard him once tell the boatswain, who was 'very much intoxicated': 'You have acted very vilely and I will not overlook it'.

Butter would not have melted in Strephon's mouth, however he was embarrassed when Frazier cross-examined him: 'Do you remember one day on the poop, that I was standing alongside of you, and the Captain was abusing the officer of the watch, did you say you never saw such behaviour on the *Spartiate's* quarter-deck, when Sir Francis Laforey commanded her and we belonged to her?' Strephon stuck to his guns, however, maintaining that he had not meant what was implied, and that though Bligh often said, 'Sir, you have not done your duty', he did not remember his ever making use of 'ungentlemanlike language'. Strephon was the most unconvincing witness of the lot.

Finally, William Simmons, another of Bligh's witnesses, denied that Bligh had called him 'a long pelt of a bitch' or, at least, not to his knowledge. Though the captain was 'sometimes passionate and sometimes very cool', he would as soon sail with Captain Bligh as with any other captain.

Bligh, in his own defence, admitted to 'ebullition of the mind' when he found dereliction of duty amongst his officers. He said that Frazier was a man of 'notoriously worthless and profligate manners' who had made efforts to stir up witnesses against him, who had often evaded his duty, and had made fun of his captain 'with sarcastic gestures' when church services were being held.

Altogether, the trial bore the marks of an affair which had been drummed up by Frazier, supported by three other resentful lieutenants, in an attempt to exploit Bligh's *Bounty* reputation. No doubt he was a trying commander as the surgeon's mate said, 'rather abusive and irritating'—but it seems that most accepted his manner with a philosophic shrug, especially in the lower ranks.

Béchervaise, in his book *Farewell,* quoted an old shellback who had spent his life in service on the Lower Deck. His testimony could well apply to Captain Bligh.

'I would always choose a ship in which every duty was attended to strictly, in preference to one in which a man did almost as he liked. Indeed, I've frequently heard old seamen say . . . "I'll go with Captain ——: he's a taut one, but he is Captain of his own ship"'.

CHAPTER XII

Governor Bligh

The *Warrior* court martial was over on February 26, 1805. It had apparently been regarded as a trivial affair in official circles, for, only a few weeks later, Sir Joseph Banks recommended Bligh for the governorship of New South Wales. This was the greatest challenge presented to Bligh in his career, and he spent some time in coming to his decision.

The letter which he received from Banks was flattering. Banks described how he had been unofficial adviser to the government on all matters concerning New South Wales since the colony's birth, and that therefore he had been asked to recommend a successor to Governor King: 'I was this day asked if I knew a man proper to be sent out in his stead —one who has integrity unimpeached, a mind capable of providing its own resources in difficulty without leaning on others for advice, firm in discipline, civil in deportment and not subject to whimper and whine when severity of discipline is wanted to meet emergencies. I immediately answered: As this man must be chosen from among the post captains, I know of no one but Captain Bligh who will suit . . .'

Banks went on to say that, on his insistence, Bligh could expect a salary of £2,000 a year, double that of previous governors, and he added: 'To me, I confess, it appears a promising place for a man who has entered late into the status of a post-captain, and the more so as your rank will go on, for Phillip, the first Governor, is now an Admiral, holding a pension for his services in the country'.

Banks was no doubt sincere in his comments, but, reading between the lines, one imagines that Bligh was approved for this position less because of his 'unimpeached integrity' and 'civil deportment', and more because he had the reputation of being a bit of a tyrant. The colony was proving troublesome and expensive, and it was felt that previous governors had been too weak or ineffectual to solve its problems. The actual situation of the Governor was too difficult and complex to allow the simple expedient of sending out a strong man. At this stage, there should have been a full inquiry into the state of affairs in New South Wales. However, this would have involved additional expense at a time when the importance of colonial affairs everywhere was receding in the light of Napoleon's rumoured invasion. So the easy way out was taken—Bligh, like some Roman gladiator, was to be sent into the lions' den, with suitable emoluments.

Bligh's first concern was the prospect of another separation from his wife. She could not accompany him, for 'her undertaking the voyage would be her death, owing to her extreme horror of the sea'. She had not 'for these ten years past been able to . . . bear even to be on board of ship with me for a few hours'.

Also, he had no doubts about the strength of the opposition he would encounter in New South Wales.

The history of the colony to date had been an ugly one, beginning as a penal settlement ruled by the New South Wales Corps whose officers were of 'low and inferior stamp'. No soldier of merit or influence would choose a tour of duty to a remote and dismal penal colony. It is not surprising that the initial 21 officers of the Corps were a quarrelsome group from the start, always fighting and duelling over trivial matters.

Unfortunately, when the first governor, Phillip, sailed home in ill-health in 1792, the colony was left in the hands of these men. The arrival of Governor Hunter was delayed until late in 1795, and, during the interregnum, the military entrenched themselves and built up a stranglehold over the administration which Hunter and his successor, King, failed to break. They lorded it over the colony and were 'haughty and arrogant to all outside their class, from whom they expected a doffing of the cap and other visible proofs of obsequiousness'.

The officers set themselves up as merchants, wholesale and retail dealers, importing rum and all other commodities through hastily employed agents overseas, though such practice was against War Office regulations. Their pay was in fact low, and ordinarily a little modest dealing was overlooked; however, in this case, there seemed to be no end to their greed.

The officers soon became gentlemen farmers, taking grants of the choicest land, which were worked by the convicts, who were maintained at Crown expense. The officers also developed all sorts of rackets. They controlled the government store—the colony's only market— where, in later times of surplus, their own grain was bought first, the doors then being closed to other settlers. By 1800, they were by far the leading graziers of the colony, possessing most of the precious live-stock.

The wretched situation of the convicts, and of the emancipists and poor settlers struggling to farm small allotments, was cynically exploited by the officer clique. Great quantities of cheap rum were imported and re-sold for enormous profit. So large was the quantity of spirits in circulation that rum became a way of life, for the colony offered little else in the way of pleasure or panacea. 'Rum fever' was a very contagious disease, bringing with it a general state of hopelessness and degradation. It was commonplace to see a group of men sitting around a bucket of rum, drinking it out of quart pots, until they fell senseless on the ground.

Rum soon became the most common article of barter, almost a complete currency. The colony's chaplain, the Reverend Richard Johnson, found himself forced to pay part of the wages for the building of the first church in rum—despite his 'methodistical tendencies'.

The officers asserted a monopoly on all trade, by forbidding civilians to board ships in the harbour to buy goods. In 1797, the officers entered into a bond not to underbuy or undersell each other. Later, some civilians forced their way into the officer circle, but the military remained dominant. Officers had the power to expropriate the land of settlers who could not pay for the goods they were forced to buy at inflated prices. It was no use appealing to the colony's courts. Civil magistrates had been replaced by military, so the officers effectively controlled the courts. Private enterprise was now supported at the expense of government enterprise—government farms, established by Phillip, fell into a state of neglect. Individual farmers had been granted a certain number of convict servants to boost grain production at a time when the colony was starving, but as the officers gained more and more land they found that ten labourers were insufficient. So they altered the hours of public labour—ostensibly to avoid the heat—making convicts free from 9 a.m. to 4 p.m. each working day. They were then encouraged to hire themselves out to the new regime of farmers who 'not being restrained from paying for labour with spirits, got a great deal of work done on their several farms'.

In the memoirs of Joseph Holt is a graphic description of the rum system at work: 'Captain Anthony Fenn Kemp, when a soldier came to him for his month's pay, would usually accost him with "Well, what do you want?" "I want to be paid, Sir," the soldier would say. "What will you have?" was always Captain Kemp's answer. "I have very good tobacco, ten shillings the pound, and good tea at twenty shillings the pound, prints at eight shillings the yard" and so on. If the poor soldier answered, "Sir, I do not want any of your goods," the Captain's comment was "You don't; you are a damned saucy rascal . . . Begone, you damned mutinous scoundrel or I'll send you to the guard house and have you flogged for impertinence to your officer." The soldier, having no redress, would take his monthly pay in property he did not want, and then he would endeavour to dispose of what he had received to some person who had money; generally selling it for less than half the price he was charged by his Captain'.

The commanding officer of the New South Wales Corps, who became Lieutenant-Governor when Phillip left, was Major Grose. When he secured the command in 1789, he had been idle on half-pay for six years, and was debilitated by wounds received in the American War of Independence. A senior position in a corps destined for a safe tour of duty was, for him, something of a sinecure. He was amiable and lazy. He was, therefore, more than happy to hand over all administrative problems to an energetic off-sider ('my Counsellor') John Macarthur, the béte noir of every Governor from Phillip to Darling, who became the leader of the military clique.

Macarthur was neither amiable nor lazy. He had come to New South Wales with his wife because, as she said in a letter to her mother, this step gave them 'every reasonable expectation of reaping the most material advantages'. Given promotion to a captaincy, they expected to return home in a few years. As it turned out, the 'material advantages' exceeded their wildest dreams, and they stayed on. Macarthur was quick-minded and without scruple in his business dealings. He was also a teetotaller, dyspeptic and prone to rheumatism. While his brother officers debauched themselves, he brooded over real or imaginary slights and charted out strategies for making money. This son of a Plymouth draper and seller of slops now seized every opportunity to exploit the colony. Those who crossed him found that he was vindictive and insolent. The unquiet, fractious spirit of this man added much to the sum total of human misery in the founding years. In 1832 he was removed from the Legislative Council at the request of Governor Bourke on the ground of insanity; he died two years later.

Governor Hunter's efforts to curb racketeering failed, and Macarthur took the lead in a campaign to have him recalled, writing direct to the Colonial Office to criticise Hunter's administration. Hunter wrote also, declaring that 'Macarthur would be satisfied with nothing less than full powers of Governor', and that 'your complaint of want of support...can only have proceeded from my choosing to have some opinion of my own in those services for which I feel myself responsible'.

The small settlers lost faith in Hunter and sent a direct appeal to the Secretary of State in London. Hunter was recalled, defeated, in 1800.

The next governor, King, was happily rid of Macarthur for a few years, sending him back to England to face a court martial for wounding his senior officer, Paterson, in one of his frequent duels. To some extent King was able to undermine the power of the now leaderless clique. Reforms were put under way, though, like Hunter, King was faced with unceasing hostility. Anonymous letters went to London, vilifying King and his administration.

Then, in 1805, Macarthur returned. King had sent three despatches to the Colonial Office outlining the charges against Macarthur: one had been lost in a shipwreck, another had been cleverly stolen, and the arrival of the third seems to have been mysteriously delayed until after the court martial was suspended for want of witnesses.

In England, Macarthur had managed to interest woollen manufacturers in the possibility of New South Wales becoming a major source of supply, since the war with France had cut off the fine wool coming from Spain. The prospect of making an expensive colony self-supporting by setting up a new industry naturally interested the Colonial Office and government. They were eager to see Macarthur succeed, and Lord Camden gave him permission to resign from the army and to start breeding sheep full-time on a 5,000 acre grant of his own choice, with a promise of a further 5,000 acres if he could prove the commercial practicability of the industry. Macarthur's experience in sheep farming was limited, and despite some like Sir Joseph Banks, who questioned the feasibility of Macarthur's plan, the Colonial Office decided to back Macarthur. He sailed home with its blessing and several Spanish Merino sheep from the Royal flock at Kew.

Governor King asked to be relieved in 1803 because of poor health. His nerve had also failed, and for the remainder of his term he was almost obsequious towards Macarthur. In fact, before his recall, he was on the point of coming to some sort of underhand land deal, which, as Macarthur later mentioned to his wife, 'would have secured a splendid future

View of part of Parramatta, NSW. By G. W. Evans.

for both our families as he possessed the power to give me any quantity of land and any number of servants'.

So, in 1805, Macarthur was once again firmly entrenched, more powerful than ever now having influential backers and patrons in England. The rum traffic and the trading monopoly still flourished, and though Bligh would be expected to suppress these evils, he would have no means of enforcing his orders other than through the New South Wales Corps or the courts under their control.

Bligh hedged for some weeks, but the terms on which he finally accepted the appointment were very favourable to one who had always had, in Mrs Bligh's phrase, the desire 'to procure a little affluence'. The final terms were: £2,000 a year, a claim to a pension of half his salary, his rank in the navy to continue, the command of HM ships in the New South Wales station with full pay, and, finally, the chance to promote the career of his son-in-law, Putland, whom he would take with him as his lieutenant. Thus he could also take his beloved daughter, Mary, who would fill the role of Governor's Lady and make his exile more pleasant. It was also privately agreed that he would stay no longer than four years. Such an honourable opportunity for profit was, for Bligh, impossible to resist, especially as he was the father of four unmarried daughters, one at least of whom would always remain a dependant. Perhaps the challenge of the situation, which had already defeated two of his peers, also attracted the aggressive side of his nature. However, he appears a reluctant tyrant when writing to his nephew, Francis Bond, to say that the governorship 'I see will be a very arduous task to me from having Very rebellious and bad People to Govern. I fear I shall be five years absent, at the end of which I hope I shall moor myself in some quiet situation for life'.

Bligh sailed for New South Wales in February, 1806. In his instructions was the important paragraph forbidding him to allow spirits to be landed in the colony without his consent, a prohibition which was again strongly emphasised in his 'Further Instructions'. Dr Mackaness wrote that this, 'by being too scrupulously interpreted, was later to prove the cause of his downfall'.

Bligh was selected as governor because he was expected to win a simple confrontation with racketeers. Unfortunately, the British Government was not prepared to support him to the hilt when the confrontation occurred.

Old Government House at Parramatta, used as a vice-regal residence until 1855.

CHAPTER XIII

Rum Rebellion

Bligh, his daughter, and son-in-law set sail for New South Wales in February, 1806 on the *Lady Madeleine Sinclair,* in a group of merchantmen and transports convoyed by HMS *Porpoise,* commanded by Captain Short.

Bligh, driven as always by the need to defend his professional status, and possibly in bad humour at the prospect of four years of 'exile', became embroiled in a series of violent quarrels with Captain Short. Short appears to have been a match for Bligh in terms of sound and fury; but he was also somewhat incompetent and irresponsible, which made matters worse as far as Bligh was concerned.

The conflict centred on the dispute over which man had supreme command of the convoy. Each had grounds for believing that he was in the right. However, such an absurd clash would never have arisen between men of tact and goodwill. Bligh, senior in rank to Short, had been appointed first captain of the *Porpoise,* but for reasons of comfort had elected to travel with his daughter on the *Lady Sinclair.* He should have been content to hand over the reins to his junior who, for all his failings, would no doubt have got them to New South Wales safely enough.

On the other hand, Short's temper was uncontrolled, and he fell out even with his own officers, particularly Daniel Lye (whom he placed under arrest) and J. S. Tetley. His rage with Bligh culminated in an incident in which he ordered Lieutenant Putland, as officer of the watch on the *Porpoise,* to fire across the bow and stern of the *Lady Sinclair.* Mary Putland wrote to her mother: 'I think such an inhuman thing as making a man fire at his wife and father was never done before'.

[With all this violent behaviour, it is worth mentioning that, according to Michael Lewis, lunacy was the second most common disorder in the navy at that period, and that the incidence of insanity was a good deal greater among officers than men. In 1815, Sir Gilbert Blane tentatively blamed 'naval madness' on head injuries from low ceilings of ships (mostly acquired when intoxicated, he felt). But the strains and tensions of sea-life are a sufficient factor in themselves: a poor diet, overcrowding and the constant disorientation of balance due to the motion of the sea. Considering the poor conditions and the length of 18th century sea voyages, it is not surprising that there were endless examples of eccentricity, violent behaviour and personality clashes.]

Bligh was convinced that Short was a 'vicious, evil-disposed designing man' and

was not inclined to forget or forgive once on dry land. On arrival at Sydney he appointed a Court of Enquiry, which found Short guilty of breaches of discipline, including drunkenness when in command of his ship. Later, a second enquiry into Short's counter-charges against Tetley and Lye also found against him, and at the end of 1807 Bligh ordered him to England to face a court martial.

The Short case was important because by this time the Macarthur clique was already doing its best to discredit Bligh in influential circles in England. Once again, letters of complaint were sent to the home government. The Short case provided a novel opportunity for intrigue. Damaging rumours were spread, and even the unfortunate death of Short's wife and one of his children on the difficult voyage home was made to appear as a consequence of Bligh's vindictive behaviour. Sympathy was with Short, and after he was honourably acquitted in December 1807, the court took the unusual step of recommending him to the Admiralty for favourable consideration.

One story spread by Bligh's enemies was that he had persuaded Tetley and Lye, the two officers at odds with Short, to press charges against Short. Mrs Bligh, in London, gallantly took up arms on her husband's behalf, and obtained a sworn affidavit from Tetley denying Bligh's influence. After the affair was over, she wrote to Bligh in February, 1808: 'Thank God, your enemies have not gained their ends— their only wish was to have you recalled, they did not care upon what footing; if to answer charges, or to come home and defend yourself they cared not—so they made you leave N.S.Wales... They had the mortification to be told that a quarrel between a Captain and a Lieutenant was not thought a sufficient reason to recall a Governor. This has made them all very desperate... The only thing your friends are anxious about is to remove any record that may remain against you at the Admiralty, which might be a pretence hereafter to prevent your getting your Flag... The malice and cruelty of the people who were engaged in this business exceeds everything I ever thought men capable of... Now, my dear love, as all these wicked people have exposed their intentions without succeeding it will serve to put us on our guard against them'.

And, with a delightful example of her tact and loyalty: 'Mr Daysh desires me to beg you to be extremely cautious and not push things

Captain Johnston announcing the arrest of Bligh.

to extremities with anyone, for you have a great many enemies. I believe I told you that Sir Joseph said this gave him the higher opinion of your abilities'.

The irony of it all was that while Mrs Bligh was penning this letter in the pleasant belief that her husband's enemies had been temporarily foiled, Bligh was, quite unknown to her, under arrest in New South Wales.

At the time of his arrest Bligh had been Governor for only 17 months but it had soon become apparent to the Macarthur clique that they were in conflict with a man very different from the mild Governor Hunter or the vacillating Governor King. Unfortunately, Bligh became involved in total war with Macarthur, personally. Macarthur engineered the 'Rum Rebellion' to save himself from ruin. No other man in New South Wales was artful or obsessive enough to have carried it off. And Bligh was no man to avoid a personal confrontation.

As well as his usual resourcefulness and energy, Bligh had shown qualities of patience and restraint at the beginning of his term of office. He spent several months acquainting himself with the situation in the colony, and in sizing up the strength of the opposition, before making a move to end the liquor trade. He frequently entertained the Macarthurs and the military officers at Government House. Even as the breach widened, he still made conscious efforts to behave like a statesman. Mary Putland wrote to her mother in October, 1807, that 'Papa is quite well but dreadfully harrassed by business and the troublesome set of people he has to deal with. In general he gives great satisfaction, but there are a few that we suspect wish to oppose him; as yet they have done nothing openly; tho' it is known their *tools* have been at work some time; that is, they are trying to find something in Papa's conduct to write home about; but which, I am sure, from his great circumspection, they will not be able to do with honour to themselves. Mr Macarthur is one of the party, the others are the Military officers, but they are all invited to the house and treated with the same politeness as usual'.

As Bligh's relations with the monopoly trading clique worsened, his popularity with the small settlers increased. These agriculturalists were a mixed bunch, predominantly emancipists (freed convicts) who had been granted up to thirty acres on their release. The emancipists were encouraged to become farmers firstly because the production of grain on the spot would lessen the expense of the colony to the British Government, and secondly because their return to Britain would only have increased the severe unemployment problem there, which had indirectly led to their conviction in the first place. Apart from these economic reasons, there was also the pious hope that a fresh start, farming a new land, would rehabilitate many. Often it did, given perseverance and fortitude. But a large percentage of the emancipists were townspeople from the large industrial centres of Britain, ignorant of farming methods and unused to a rugged rural existence.

The British Government's vision of establishing a colony of sturdy and virtuous small-holders lost out to the Macarthur clique plan of establishing a pastoral and trading 'aristocracy'. Fourteen years after the 'Rum Rebellion' the British Government bowed to the inevitable—and the profitable—and reversed the original policy on the recommendation of Commissioner Bigge, who had been sent out to investigate the situation. (He was assiduously courted by Macarthur during his stay in New South Wales.) From 1822, well after Bligh's time, land grants were only made to those few emancipists who had capital. The difficulties facing the small-holders were glossed over, and it was maintained that they were a worthless lot, ready to sell their farms for a gallon of rum.

The 'pastoral ascendancy' after 1822 brought wealth to the country as the demands of the British textile industry for wool increased, and settlers with capital migrated to take up large tracts of land and make their fortunes.

But in Bligh's time there were few large proprietors, and the policy was still officially one of encouraging the small agriculturalist. To this end, free migrants were given assisted passages from Britain, together with land grants and the promise of assigned convict labour to help them establish themselves. Their numbers were increasing, and they became loyal Bligh supporters. Unlike some of the emancipist farmers, they tended to be sober, industrious and politically aware. They included, for instance, a group of Presbyterian settlers who took up land at Portland Head on the Hawkesbury, and co-operated in building the first Presbyterian church, at Ebenezer. They supported Bligh not only because they perceived the benefits of his administration, but also because they felt obliged to show loyalty to any 'officer whom His Majesty in His Wisdom shall think fit to appoint'.

Some settlers were concerned with the immediate material advantages which Bligh conferred upon them—one is reported to have reminisced: 'Them were the days, Sir, for the poor settler; he had only to tell the Governor what he wanted, and he was sure to get it from the Stores; whatever it was, Sir, from a needle to an anchor, from a penn'orth of pack thread to a ship's cable'.

From whatever level their loyalty sprang, Bligh earned the small farmers' support and gratitude. When he arrived, the settlers were suffering from the effects of a disastrous flooding of the Hawkesbury river. The Hawkesbury area was the main grain producing area, and the whole colony was affected. The price of wheat and maize spiralled on the open market; the government had to reduce its rations to convicts; and the spectre of famine haunted the settlement. The Hawkesbury farmers were the worst hit, of course; while endeavouring to make good their losses of livestock and possessions, they were faced with the sudden rise in food prices. Bligh immediately set to work to alleviate their distress. He toured the settled areas, gaining a first-hand knowledge of the farmers and their individual needs, and he gave meat from government-owned cattle to those who were near starvation. Then he enabled all farmers to have their corn ground for free at the government mill, provided that they donated every eleventh bushel to distressed settlers.

The Hawkesbury farmers responded with a congratulatory address, which referred to Bligh's 'superior understanding, knowledge and ability'. They complained of some aspects of Governor King's rule, and urged specific reforms: freedom of trade in an open market, the suppression of monopolies and extortion, stabilization of currency and an end to the domination of the colony's courts by the military class.

They complained also that John Macarthur had signed a welcome address to Bligh on behalf of the free inhabitants of the colony, without their authority: 'We beg to observe that had we deputed anyone, John Macarthur would not have been chosen by us, we considering him an unfit person to step forward upon such an occasion, as we may chiefly attribute the rise in the price of mutton to his withholding the large flock of wethers he now has to make such price as he may choose to command.'

Bligh encouraged settlers to increase the acreage under cultivation by promising them that the Government Store would buy all surplus wheat at a good price at the next harvest. He brought in new regulations to reduce the cost of labour, and he allowed the most destitute settlers to take articles they needed from the Government Store on extended credit. The Store contained all the simple necessities of life at a reasonable price— three or four times lower than the prices offered by private traders.

In January 1807 the Hawkesbury settlers thanked Bligh in a second address for rescuing them from 'the dreadful crisis', and gave a significant assurance that 'under a just and benign Government, we will be ready at all times, at the risque of our lives and properties, to support the same'.

They added: 'We have subscribed all the grain we conveniently can spare from our own support to be carried to the public stores at your stipulated price, rejecting far greater prices in money which we could receive at the present market sale'. Bligh had encouraged them to sell to the Government Store, in spite of competitive prices offered by private traders —but it was in their own interest to do so both in order to maintain their credit with the Store and to avoid forcing Bligh into the 'ruinous necessity of importation' of grain.

In October 1807 he informed the Secretary of State of his measures to improve farming practices. He encouraged the use of the plough, allowing Government oxen to be bought for this purpose, and enacted certain rules to prevent over-cropping. By selling government livestock at reduced prices he hoped to encourage the settlers 'not only to plough, but to manure and fence in their grounds, which I have earnestly recommended, and will become a general system in due time'.

Bligh's measures were ingenious and practical, but his anti-profiteering policies threatened those who 'could no longer sell the usual quantity of Bengal rum, Brazil's tobacco, Siam sugar, Young Hyson tea, or British manufactured goods at the usual remunerating prices'.

The Hawkesbury settlers signed two more loyal addresses to Bligh before his arrest, and sent a number of pro-Bligh petitions to London afterwards. At this time Bligh's close associates were imprisoned or under surveillance by the rebels, so the petitions were likely to have been spontaneous and genuine.

Portrait of John Macarthur, leader of the clique opposed to Governor Bligh.

Mrs Elizabeth Macarthur, wife of John Macarthur.

'What have I to do with your sheep—Sir?'
Bligh v Macarthur as seen by Norman Lindsay.

Elizabeth Farm, home of the Macarthurs.

Bligh had other links with the Hawkesbury district which were not so creditable. On Bligh's arrival in Sydney, there occurred an improper land transaction between himself and Governor King. While King was still in office, he granted Bligh three parcels of land, the largest—1000 acres—being in the Hawkesbury district. When Bligh took office four days later, he at once reciprocated, granting 790 acres to King's wife. This property was imprudently named 'Thanks'.

None of these grants were mentioned in despatches, though for grants of this size the approval of the Secretary of State should have been sought. (After Bligh's death their validity was questioned, but his son-in-law compromised with the Crown by surrendering one property and retaining the other two.)

Then Bligh erred again in using convict servants—fed and clothed at government expense—and government livestock and stores to develop another property he owned. Bligh claimed that this was intended as a 'model farm' to demonstrate efficient farming methods to the settlers. He also maintained that he intended to pay for government supplies and would have done so had he not been deposed.

However a demonstration of efficient farming could better have been carried out on one of the neglected public farms. Bligh's farm was very profitable to him. As his bailiff, Andrew Thompson, said: 'It may be observed that a common farmer who has to pay for everything would by no means have such profits'.

Bligh's opportunism does not compare with the scale of exploitative activities of the Macarthur clique. But, of course, by using the privilege of his office for profit he undermined the authority of the Governorship and made it easier for his enemies to discredit him.

In the first six months, while keeping one eye on the liquor trade and its sorry effects, he busied himself with innocuous reforms. He diverted convict labour to repair dilapidated public buildings, including Government House itself; and started work on unfinished churches at Sydney and Parramatta. The government surveyor was requested to draw up a plan to improve the appearance of Sydney town. 'When I have done I think it will be a very charming place', he wrote. The education of the 'currency lads and lasses'—as the first generations of native born Australians were called—also concerned Bligh, and soon he was able to report that nearly four hundred children were receiving tuition throughout the colony.

Bligh observed on the reign of corruption that existed: 'A sawyer will cut one hundred feet of timber for a bottle of spirits, value 2/6d, which he drinks in a few hours; when for the same labor he would charge two bushels of wheat which would furnish bread for him for two months; hence those who have got no liquor to pay their laborers with, are ruined by paying more than they can profitably afford ...while those who have liquor gain an immense advantage ... those who have got spirits go or send their agents to purchase wheat, and frequently take from the thoughtless settler two or three bushels of wheat for a bottle of spirits ... On this account principally it is that the farmers are involved in debt, and either ruined by the high price of spirits or the high price of labor which is regulated thereby; while the unprincipled holder of spirits has work done at a cheap rate and amasses considerable property'.

In February 1807 Bligh threw down the gauntlet, challenging the combined group of military and non-military traders with a general order prohibiting absolutely the exchange of rum or any other liquor for food, grain, labour, clothes and all other commodities. As he wrote to the Colonial Secretary, Windham: 'I am aware that prohibiting the barter of spirits will meet with the marked opposition of those few who have so materially enriched themselves by it'.

The tactics of the opposition to reform were master-minded by Macarthur, and involved a self-righteous stance in the name of liberty on a public level, and a smear campaign and cheap insults on a more underhand level. The common soldiers of the New South Wales Corps were incited by their officers to undermine Bligh's authority in petty ways—for instance, laughing out loud when Bligh appeared at church in full uniform.

Bligh's rough quarter deck manner, and the reputation he had acquired from the *Bounty* mutiny, made him an easy target for ridicule. Macarthur claimed that he had been rebuffed rudely by Bligh at one of their earliest meetings, when Macarthur had irritated the Governor by asking some favour or other. Bligh had turned on him: 'What have I to do with your sheep, Sir? What have I to do with your cattle? Are you to have such flocks of sheep and such herds of cattle as no man ever heard of before? No, Sir, I have heard of your concerns, Sir, you have got 5000 acres of land, Sir, in the finest situation in the country, but by God you shan't keep it'. When Macarthur smugly reminded him that the land had been granted by the Secretary of State on recommendation from the Privy Council, Bligh roared: 'Damn the Privy Council, and damn the Secretary of State too; he commands at home, I command here!' Bligh later denied this story.

Now in earnest, the conflicts often ended up in court, for, as Dr Evatt comments: 'the courts were the true forum of the little colony' in the lack of organized political parties, and independent press. Also the military officers had effective control of the criminal court, which consisted of six officers sitting with the Judge-Advocate to make up the statutory tribunal of seven. (Not that verdicts were always a foregone conclusion, as the officers were always falling out with each other.) In this situation, the character and ability of the Judge-Advocate were extremely important.

Richard Atkins, who had held the position of Judge-Advocate since 1796, was from an influential aristocratic family. He was well educated and 'polished', but was so fond of good living that he had already dissipated a large inheritance by the time he was 21. As his alcoholism asserted itself, he was so beset by creditors that he sold his military commission and took his family to New South Wales. Atkins was one of the first of a long line of 'remittance men' from influential families, who, like the convicts 'left their country for their country's good'.

As the colonists were not aware of the background to his arrival, his good connections and aristocratic manner were sufficient reason for Governor Phillip to appoint him a Justice of the Peace in 1792. In Governor Hunter's time, his weakness for alcohol—which often made him ill—was no longer a secret, but Hunter knew his family personally and despite his conduct and his lack of legal knowledge, fostered his elevation to the office of Judge-Advocate. By 1802, an exasperated Governor King was writing to Lord Hobart: 'As so much information and assistance to the Governor is required of the person who acts in that situation, I humbly suggest to your Grace's consideration the propriety of a person having some general knowledge of the law and a fair character, being sent here to fill that important situation as soon as possible'.

By the end of Bligh's first year, Atkins had fathered a couple of illegitimate children, his house was 'a perfect pigstye', his life was described by Surgeon Harris as 'worse than

a dog's' and he had a reputation for coming drunk into court and sentencing prisoners to death for minor thefts. Bligh was not one to stand in awe of Atkins's family, and he wrote to Banks that the authorities should remove Atkins without delay, since he was 'very unfit and very disgraceful', a 'disgrace to human jurisprudence'. Bligh also reported to Windham that he would have replaced Atkins had there been anyone else willing or able to serve as Judge-Advocate in the colony. The failure of the British Government to send out a suitable person in his place meant that Bligh had to rely on this weak reed in his hour of crisis.

The first open breach between Macarthur and Bligh was a result of Macarthur's suit against Andrew Thompson, Bligh's own bailiff. When the price of wheat had been low, Macarthur had accepted a promissory note from Thompson for a sum of money which was expressed on the note in bushels of wheat, according to local custom. Macarthur called up the note when the price of wheat had spiralled after the floods, and refused to accept Thompson's offer to pay wheat equal to its value at the time the note was issued. The Civil Court decided against Macarthur; Macarthur appealed to Bligh and Bligh immediately dismissed the appeal. From that time, Macarthur ceased his visits to Government House; though Bligh characteristically harboured no burning resentment. He enquired kindly after Macarthur during a brief illness, and called upon Mrs Macarthur on an occasion when the master of the house was conspicuous by his absence.

In July the Macarthur faction was further annoyed when Bligh suspended the rich and influential D'Arcy Wentworth, from his post as assistant surgeon. Bligh was striking a blow at those who used unauthorized convict labour for their own profit. In this, the medical officers were as guilty as the military, for it was proved that Wentworth had used 'convalescents' on the books of his hospital as workers on his farm and private garden. Bligh may seem to have over-reacted, especially considering his own use of convict labour.

In October there was another direct confrontation between Macarthur and Bligh over an imported still. Due to the insatiable thirst of the colony, profiteers were always tempted to make 'moonshine' liquor illegally, and in March the ship *Dart* had arrived in Sydney Harbour carrying two stills for this purpose—one for Captain Abbott and one (larger) for Macarthur. Since Bligh had forbidden the importation of stills, he ordered them to be seized and kept in the Government Store until they could be shipped back to England. The Naval Officer was a friend of Macarthur, however, and allowed him to take the copper boilers out of the stores—the excuse being that a supply of medicine was packed in them. The boilers were the vital parts of the stills— the heads and worms which remained in the Store could have been manufactured in the colony. When Bligh heard of this, he gave instructions that the boilers should be handed back into custody. In May Bligh dismissed the Naval Officer and installed one of his own friends in the position.

The division opening up in the colony was not merely one between Bligh united with the poorer settlers against the officers and their associates. Bligh had some influential colonists on his side, too. Robert Campbell, a sober Scot and the first independent merchant in New South Wales, was one. He gave extensive credit and fair trade, and in 1804 had been presented with a grateful memorial from two hundred settlers: 'But for you, we had still been a prey to the Mercenary unsparing Hand of Avarice and Extortion'.

Bligh found him 'a just, humane and a gentleman-like merchant' and it was not surprising that he was preferred over one of Bligh's enemies as that Naval Officer in charge of customs.

Five months later, the *Duke of Portland* was about to sail for London, and Bligh ordered that both stills, complete, should be shipped back to the agent who originally sent them out. In other words, Bligh was not confiscating the stills, but permitting their exportation for resale in London.

Macarthur quibbled that he wanted to sell his in India or China, or else keep the copper boiler for 'some domestic use'. Bligh had to instruct Campbell to take the stills 'on Governor's orders'. Campbell sent his nephew to do the deed, and Macarthur immediately prosecuted him for illegal seizure of property. The case was complicated by the fact that the nephew had no official status, and gave no receipt to Macarthur. Because of this loophole Macarthur won the case, partly owing to Atkins's weakness and ignorance of the law. Bligh's actions, according to Dr Evatt, were clearly in the right.

Macarthur was no doubt elated by the verdict, which encouraged him to press on with the anti-Bligh campaign. He enjoyed appearing before his friends in the court, puffed

up with hollow but impressive-sounding rhetoric designed to inflame colonial feelings. His performance on this occasion had been a masterpiece of hypocrisy:

'It would therefore appear that a British subject, living in a British settlement, in which the British laws are established by the Royal Patent, has had his property wrested from him by a non-accredited individual, without any authority being produced...then that it was the Governor's order. It is therefore for you, gentlemen, to determine whether this be the tenor on which Englishmen hold their property in New South Wales?'

Macarthur had not long to wait for his next opportunity to malign Bligh. It was found that a convict had escaped on one of his trading ships, and some English missionaries in Tahiti complained that this 'notorious character' had left ship there and was causing trouble amongst the Tahitians. Such stowaways were common, and in an effort to have ships

Campbell's wharf, Sydney Cove. Robert Campbell was the first independent merchant in NSW and one of Bligh's most loyal supporters.

effectively searched before leaving Sydney a regulation was in force which obliged shipowners to lodge a bond for £800 with the Government, until the authorities could ascertain that no convicts had hidden on the outgoing vessel.

When the *Parramatta* returned to Sydney, the ship was placed under arrest and the crew was questioned. Since there was no doubt that the convict had been concealed and found on board, the bond given by Macarthur and his partner Blaxcell was declared to be forfeited. Macarthur's response was provocative. He informed the crew of the *Parramatta* that he had abandoned the ship and would no longer be responsible for their pay and provisions. The crew were thus forced ashore, breaking a regulation which prohibited unauthorized landing. As Bligh put it, the men were 'thrown upon the public without support'. When Macarthur refused to answer for his action, a warrant was served to bring him before the

bench of magistrates. But Macarthur handed this written reply to the constable who went to arrest him: 'Mr Oakes—You will inform the persons who sent you here with the warrant...that I never will submit to the horrid tyranny that is attempted until I am forced; that I consider it with scorn and contempt, as I do the persons who have directed it to be executed'.

Macarthur's defiance now placed him in a dangerous situation, for next morning he was arrested and this time committed for trial before the Criminal Court. Macarthur still had an opportunity for further manoeuvres and defiance. He erected a fence around a disputed leasehold in the heart of the town, compelling Bligh to tear it down again, and he formally objected to Atkins's sitting in judgement upon him, on the grounds that Atkins owed him a small amount of money, and was an old enemy.

Probably Macarthur received assurance of support from most of the officers who were to try him; to curry favour with the Corps he purchased a quantity of cheap wine and offered to retail it to non-commissioned officers at unusually generous rates.

On the night before the trial, in 'an act of brazen effrontery', the anti-Bligh faction—with the exception of Macarthur himself—assembled at a mess dinner, complete with wine and music. Colonel Johnston, the commanding officer, tumbled out of his chaise on the way home.

A large crowd, mostly soldiers, assembled at the court on the following morning. Before the trial could proceed, Macarthur rose and made an impassioned speech objecting to Atkins's presiding over the court and accusing him of being in a conspiracy 'to deprive me of my property, honour and life'. Since he would certainly have been acquitted by the other six officers, this could only have been another attempt to confront Bligh's administration in an inflammatory way. But in the midst of uproar Atkins adjourned the court and retreated to Government House. The six officers sent a note to Bligh informing him that they would not sit with Atkins; and their commanding officer refused Bligh's subsequent summons to confer with him at Government House, on the feeble grounds of his minor accident the night before.

However, Macarthur was re-arrested and put into gaol by the 'loyalist' Provost-Marshal, Gore, early next morning. The situation became farcical when the six officers re-assembled, announced that they were functioning as a court, and that they intended to challenge Gore's action. The officers now were as deeply implicated as Macarthur himself. Of course, all would have been acquitted in a court dominated by their own faction. But when Bligh summoned each of the six to attend him at nine o'clock on the following morning, they feared that Bligh might act against them through his loyal civil magistrates instead, sitting with himself as a sort of grand jury. Obviously, Bligh would have to be deposed immediately, and they could now say that rebellion was necessary—for wasn't the tyrant subverting the laws of the land?

In the evening, the news aroused Major Johnston from his retreat in a 'temporary forgetfulness of my bruises'. He ordered Macarthur's release, and consulted with him at the barracks. At his trial in England in 1811, Johnston claimed that 'an immense number of people, comprising all the respectable inhabitants, except those who were immediately connected with Captain Bligh, rushed into the barracks & surrounded me, repeating with importunate clamour a solicitation that I would immediately place the Governor under arrest. They solemnly assured me, if I did not, an insurrection & massacre would certainly take place; & added that the blood of the colonists would be upon my head...& it was urged among other things, that the arrest of the Governor would be the preservation of his life, as the popular fury would first burst upon him & his agents'.

According to the Macarthur records, Johnston cried: 'God's curse! What am I to do, Macarthur, here are these fellows advising me to arrest the Governor', to which Macarthur replied, 'Advising you; then, Sir, the only thing left for you to do is to do it. To advise on such matters is legally as criminal as to do them'. And then Macarthur, on a gun in the barrack square, wrote the petition to Johnston... a requisition for Bligh's arrest.

This, according to Johnston, was no sooner laid upon the table than it 'was filled with as many signatures as it could contain'. However, it emerged at the trial that the requisition was signed only by six or seven men at most *before* the arrest—other signatures were obtained later, when the rebels were in power. Moreover, it is not to be believed that the inhabitants of

Sydney, other than the Macarthur clique, were clamouring for Bligh's arrest, let alone fearing insurrection and massacre. Johnston on his arrival at the barrack would have been met by the officers of the Corps and a few interested profiteers and opportunists who urged and persuaded him to usurp the government of the colony. Johnston 'immediately ordered the Corps under Arms, and directed four Officers to proceed to Government House and summon Governor Bligh to resign his Authority'.

The regiment marched the few hundred yards to Government House, colours flying and the band 'playing "The British Grenadiers" and other lively tunes', accompanied by Macarthur and friends and a gaggle of curious citizenry.

Bligh was dining with five 'loyalists' including Campbell, Palmer the Commissary (whose sister Campbell had married) and Atkins. Later, one of them described the scene: Atkins left the dinner table to reconnoitre events at the barrack, and returned saying: 'There is a great movement in Barrack-square, and the military are all under arms'. Bligh said, 'Surely they dare not attack my person?' To which Atkins replied, 'I have no doubt but that they will'. Bligh poured out a glass of wine, and rising (with great trepidation) said, 'The health of the King!' He then drank off the wine and left the table.

At this time, both Bligh and Mary Putland were in mourning, for Lieutenant Putland had died of consumption two weeks before. (Incidentally, Colonel Johnston had attended the funeral as chief official mourner; a memory which increased Bligh's bitterness.)

Bligh had two motives for retiring so precipitously from the table. First—rather characteristically—he went upstairs to change from his drab suit of mourning into full uniform. If he was to be arrested, he was determined that it would be in fitting style and so he pinned his Camperdown medal to his breast. Second, he called for important papers and documents, some of which he managed to conceal beneath his waistcoat, others which he destroyed on the spot. However he had no time to save them all— the rebels later rummaged upstairs and downstairs and seized the remainder, in an effort— as Bligh later affirmed—'to find matter of crimination against me; to defend the mutinous act; and to deprive me of that assistance those papers would have afforded'. (Also, some confidential letters to the Secretary of State contained some plain speaking about certain colonial characters—Bligh was later embarrassed by an account he had written of Atkins, which the rebels gleefully revealed to the latter.)

By now, three or four hundred soldiers with loaded muskets were surrounding Government House. Mrs Putland, who had grasped her parasol, 'hastened to the gates & gallantly opposed their entrance, setting the bayonets at defiance and exclaiming "you traitors, you rebels, you have just walked over my husband's grave & now come to murder my father".' According to this eye-witness, 'she continued until forcibly dragged away—but again escaped nor would she be opposed'.

Johnston proceeded into the house with a party of soldiers, breaking in without ceremony, and arrested all the 'loyalists' present downstairs. At this point Bligh decided that he was not going to give himself up easily—a decision no doubt motivated by stubborn anger rather than cowardice. He therefore concealed himself in a tiny servant's room. There was a chance, he said later, that 'he could possibly get clear of the troops and get to the Hawkesbury' during the night, where the loyal settlers would have rallied around him. Certainly he had nothing to lose by playing for time. Had his concealment been successful, the New South Wales Corps would have looked very foolish indeed, and his supporters might have had a chance to engineer a counter-rebellion. As it was, the soldiers took well over an hour to find him.

The rebels later used his concealment as evidence of cowardice, which was perhaps the unkindest cut of all. The three soldiers who found him claimed that he was hiding under a bed in terror, and was dragged out all covered in feathers, pleading for his life. However their stories at Johnston's trial contained glaring discrepancies, and one broke down under cross-examination, confessing that he did not even recollect whether there was a feather bed in the room or not. (Bligh wrote to his nephew after the trial 'You must bear in mind that no feather bed was in the House . . .').

The story that Bligh was found in a craven condition was useful propaganda, and a crude cartoon of the event was circulated, making Bligh an object of ridicule. Bligh scornfully denied the charge of cowardice at the trial: 'Was it for me then to sully my reputation and to disgrace the medal I wear by shrinking from death, which I have braved in every shape?'

Marcus Clarke wrote in 1890: 'His very vices were those which spring from an overweening self-confidence, combined with strong personal courage. It is not likely that a captain who had fought his ship so as to merit the thanks of Nelson, and had lived through a voyage such as that which followed upon the mutiny of the *Bounty,* would hide beneath a bed to escape from the violence of officers who had dined at his own table . . . The revolution was after all but a civil matter. There was no infuriated mob waiting to tear him to pieces. No threats of personal violence had been used; and Bligh must have known that his life was never in danger . . . the story is, in itself, precisely one of those coarse lies which are so easily invented and so readily believed by the vulgar sort'.

After his arrest, Bligh was informed that he had been deposed, and left under guard in the house while—according to one witness—'the soldiers and mob placed Macarthur in a chair and carried him about the town in a disorderly triumphant manner'.

Gore described the scene vividly: 'Liquor was liberally and indeed profusely, served to the soldiers; bonfires blazed in all parts of the town; and those scenes of riots, tumult, and insubordination that are ever incident to the subversion of legitimate government and authority ensued. McArthur, the hero of the day, paraded the streets, in the most publick parts of which he was always conspicuous; and those individuals who had not lighted their houses were compelled to illuminate them by the sergeant-major and some chosen soldiers, who were detached on that particular service. The most insulting conduct and epithets were encouraged by the junto to be applied to the Governor and to his faithful officers, and such of his adherents as had persisted in refusing to exhibit outward demonstrations of their joy and approbation were carefully marked as the victims of future prosecution'.

Macarthur found time to send a note out of town to his wife, cloaking his self-interested actions in noble rhetoric: 'I have been deeply engaged all this day in contending for the liberties of this unhappy Colony, and I am happy to say I have succeeded beyond what I expected . . . The Tyrant is now no doubt gnashing his teeth with vexation at his overthrow. May he often have cause to do the like!'

CHAPTER XIV

Bligh a Prisoner

The 'Rum Rebellion' took place on January 26, 1808. But Bligh did not embark for England until April 27, 1810. During these two years he was under the most severe strain. For nearly 14 months he was confined to Government House and its small garden, with sentries posted at the gates and doors—he was 'very much annoyed with the sentinels, who, constantly heated with liquor, seemed to have been directed to bellow "All's well" with peculiar tones of hellish composition'.

The only weapons allowed him were pen and paper, which he employed diligently. So did his friends, and, of course, the rebels themselves. A barrage of charges, counter-charges and petitions crossed the ocean slowly to England. The rebels managed to ensure that their version of events would be the first to arrive. Macarthur's son presented their despatch in London in September, 1808, but Viscount Castlereagh, who was Secretary of State for War as well as for the Colonies, declined to take much notice. Britain was totally involved in the progress of the great war on the continent. How fortunate for the rebels! At any other moment in history, it is hard to believe that Bligh would not have been quickly avenged, if not for his own sake, then for the sake of the authority of the King. War and national peril made colonial problems peripheral, necessarily solved as quickly as possible. It was decided that Johnston would have to be brought home to be court-martialled. In view of the many complaints against him, Bligh would also have to attend the trial. This would involve an absence from the colony of at least a year, so the simplest procedure would be to appoint another governor immediately. This was unfair to Bligh, and his friend Banks protested strongly when he heard of the decision. But it was reasoned that feelings ran so high in the colony that Bligh could not return to govern with any prospect of happiness to himself or advantage to the colonists. The most constructive feature of the new plan was the decision to replace the New South Wales Corps and send out a military governor, who at least could expect to command the loyalty of his own troops. The line of naval governors was ended with the appointment of Brigadier-General Nightingall to the post.

On April 16, 1809, Banks wrote to placate a distraught Mrs Bligh: 'The Government have not altered their intention of recalling your husband. Good often arises out of evil. His conduct, always in my opinion honourable,

just and equitable, has more than once been canvassed in his absence, where he has been unjustly, indecently and scandalously misused. Unfortunate as we are in the unwise decision of His Majesty's Ministers to recall him, this evil must produce the good consequences of his being able to answer for himself such charges as may be brought against him'.

The new governor's departure was delayed as it was rumoured at the Colonial Office that Bligh himself was about to arrive in England. Then, Nightingall had second thoughts about his career, and after much indecision, declined the appointment. Lieutenant-Colonel Lachlan Macquarie, the commandant of the 73rd Regiment (chosen to replace the New South Wales Corps), sailed as governor in his place. It took Macquarie seven months to reach Sydney Cove. Such was the tyranny of distance.

While the Governor of the Cape of Good Hope was entertaining Macquarie's leisurely entourage at a ball in September 1809, Castlereagh received a report compiled by T. G. Harris on the legal aspects of the rebellion, which expressed the opinion that the rebels were guilty of treason. But in the same month, as luck would have it, Castlereagh fought his famous duel with Canning and was forced to resign his position. As Macarthur wrote to his wife: 'How it might have been had Lord Castlereagh and that northern bear, Mr Cook, remained in office I cannot say; for certain it is they had both declared themselves adverse to us—and had they retained their authority they would have increased our difficulties, and perhaps, in the end, have crushed us altogether'.

While his fate was being decided, Bligh fretted and fumed in captivity. Johnston proclaimed himself Lieutenant-Governor, but Macarthur, as Colonial Secretary, was acknowledged as the real 'Ruler' of the rebel administration. All 'loyalist' civil officers and magistrates were replaced by supporters of the rebellion, and the new regime baptized itself with a special church service, inviting all citizens 'to join in thanks to Almighty God for his merciful interposition in their favour, by relieving them, without bloodshed, from the awful situation in which they stood before the memorable 26th instant'.

Macarthur, officially still facing the previous charges against him, then staged what can only be described as a mock trial. He was, of course, acquitted. The trial gave him the opportunity to vilify Bligh and his administra-

Sir Maurice Charles O'Connell who married Bligh's widowed daughter, Mrs Mary Putland, in 1810 when he was commander of the 73rd regiment and Lieutenant-Governor.

Lady Mary O'Connell, Bligh's daughter, who accompanied him as Governor's Lady to NSW. She gave Bligh all her devotion and support during the rebellion and the months of exile which followed in Tasmania.

Governor Lachlan Macquarie, who followed Bligh as Governor.

tion, which he did partly in an effort to stop a growing antipathy towards himself. Some settlers immediately signed a petition addressed to Johnston when Macarthur's appointment as Colonial Secretary reached their ears: 'We believe John McArthur has been the scourge of this colony by fomenting quarrels between His Majesty's officers, servants and subjects. His monopoly and extortion have been highly injurious to the inhabitants of every description.

'We most earnestly pray that the said John McArthur may be removed from the said office of Colonial Secretary, from all other offices, and from all public councils and interference with the government of this colony'.

The rebels circulated petitions on their own behalf. There were four pro-Johnston petitions as against seven pro-Bligh over the two years in which Bligh was held prisoner. But while the latter seem to have been spontaneous and genuine, since the signatories risked personal reprisal, the rebels could provide little evidence of mass support. One pro-Johnston document sent to the Colonial Office, for instance, contained the signatures of 66 Hawkesbury settlers, including some of the most solid and respectable farmers. But later a group of Hawkesbury residents swore that men 'heated with wine' had forced people to sign this 'treasonable and seditious document'. Another maintained that they had been threatened with the withdrawal of convict labour from their farms. And even one of the men who had solicited signatures withdrew his own name from the petition and confessed his guilty conscience to Bligh himself.

As for the most important document of the rebels, the requisition to Johnston to arrest Bligh, one discontented member of the Macarthur faction went so far as to state that not even one signature had been obtained before Bligh's arrest. Others claimed that they were forced to sign it afterwards at bayonet point.

On the day after Macarthur's trial, a large public meeting was called by the rebels at which Macarthur was elected as delegate to go to England and state the rebels' case. He thanked them for this honour, for which, 'in gratitude to his friends, he would devote the last hour of his existence to their service'. The account of his speech given in the Bligh papers says that he presented himself to the audience as 'a man who had nearly fallen a victim to a band of bloody-minded (or bloodthirsty) wretches . . . that plans, the most diabolical, had been laid with such damnable craft that could not have failed to overwhelm him in total ruin and destruction had it not been for the timely intervention of Divine Providence in rescuing him from the malice of his enemies'.

After the meeting, 'great quantities of wine and spirits were distributed by Mr Macarthur to the soldiers and populace'.

To the rest of the world, this revolution was insignificant, and scarcely worthy of notice. But even this bloodless affair followed the pattern of greater revolutions. Both sides were quick to draw parallels with events in France, accusing each other of 'Robespierrian' tactics. Bligh of course maintained that the rebels were guilty of high treason, and the rebels, in their first dispatch to Castlereagh dated April 11, 1808, claimed that Bligh had 'acted upon a predetermined plan to subvert the laws of the country, to terrify and influence the Courts of Justice, and to bereave those persons who had the misfortune to be obnoxious to him of their fortunes, their liberty, and their lives'. Then, a pattern of persecution of the supporters of the old regime began. Many were arrested and imprisoned. Provost-Marshal Gore was sentenced to seven years at the convict settlement at Newcastle on a trumped-up charge of perjury. At his trial he refused to plead, declaring to the rebel tribunal: 'You are an unlawful assembly, and illegally constituted; the most disgraceful, the most rigorous sentence you can pronounce on me I shall receive as the greatest honour you can confer on me . . .' An important witness for Gore was, before the trial, 'abruptly seized and taken by a constable from his dinner and sent to the Coal River as a place of punishment'.

George Crossley, a convict attorney upon whose advice both Bligh and Atkins, in their ignorance of the law, had leant rather too heavily for the rebels' liking, was also transported for seven years.

Settlers loyal to Bligh refused to be intimidated, and five were imprisoned for defiance. The free migrants led a protest campaign. The few emancipist farmers who joined them were noted for being 'sober and steadfast individuals who possessed a sense of civic responsibility which later led them to play an active part in the affairs of their locality', according to a study by B. H. Fletcher.

George Suttor, a free settler and a protege of Sir Joseph Banks, who had felt that his knowledge of botany and agriculture would be of value in the colony, was a leader among the Hawkesbury settlers. In August 1808, Bligh received their address expressing loyalty and gratitude, and announcing that Suttor and one other settler would go to London to inform His Majesty's Ministers of 'the rise and progress of abuses in the colony', and to assure them that the settlers were innocent of rebellion, their signatures having been obtained 'under threats, terrors, and menaces'. The settlers would collectively contribute towards the expenses of the journey.

Three months later, Suttor was in gaol. At his trial, like Gore, he refused to make a plea: 'I deny the legality of this court. My allegiance is due to Governor Bligh, and Governor Bligh alone; and every drop of blood within my veins prevents me from ever acknowledging the legality of this court. You may do with me as you think proper'.

It is interesting to note that the free settlers who became most prominent in Bligh's defence had not been on close terms with him, nor had they been given any special favours.

Another loyalist of good character, who persisted in defying the rebels though he had received no personal benefits from Bligh, was the Rev. Henry Fulton. Fulton had been transported from Ireland for political involvement, and was now temporarily chaplain of the colony. He was suspended from office by Major Johnston for introducing a prayer for Bligh into the service. One of the settlers' petitions to London complained that religion had suffered disastrously in the colony by the silencing of the only regular clergyman.

'Little Jack' Palmer, the commissary, remained in his post until he too was imprisoned in March, 1809. He drew up three separate reports which detailed the rebels' system of speculation, including the free distribution of the government cattle to the military and their associates, the resumption of the rum trade, the misuse of government stores and manipulation of receipts, and the revival of the old monopoly of all imports for the benefit of the rebel traders. In April, 1808, Bligh brooded on their iniquities: 'They have issued the stores wantonly and improperly to their private purposes; they have sold a large ten-oared boat which was kept for the Governor's use; they are giving away and disposing of Government cattle to their own party; they have renewed and given leases of several places in the town; they are employing in their private concerns artificers and labourers and Government cattle . . . They have even sold from the store three pairs of mill-stones which were intended to be sent to the out-settlements, and McArthur has taken two pair of them to himself, as likewise thirty stand of arms, which there is no doubt were sent in the *Parramatta* to barter for pork in the South Seas, and their vessels have been fitted out with the canvass and sails of His Majesty's ships'.

Soon the rebels fell out with each other, and formed into hostile factions. Some military officers and certain civilians—the Blaxland brothers and the powerful emancipist trader, Simeon Lord—felt that their rewards for supporting Bligh's arrest were rather too slow in coming. Macarthur, as unofficial ruler, was manipulating circumstances to his own advantage but was not portioning out the land grants and privileges which they felt to be their due. Johnston and Macarthur faced open hostility, and when Lieutenant-Colonel Foveaux arrived in the colony in July to take over the Lieutenant-Governorship, as Johnston's senior officer, Macarthur was dropped from the rebel administration altogether.

Bligh hoped that Foveaux might re-instate him, but Foveaux supported his old friends in the Corps, announcing that it was 'beyond his authority to judge between Captain Bligh and the officer whom he found in command of the colony'. Bligh was left under arrest, raging about this new mutiny of 'so black a hue as all England must indignantly bring the principal actors to condign punishment'.

Foveaux was the son of a French cook employed by an English earl. He had arrived in New South Wales with the Corps in 1790, and later at Norfolk Island he was known amongst convicts as the man who laughed when they begged for mercy during a flogging, and who ordered so many lashes for one man that his shoulder blades were exposed like 'two ivory polished horns'. He had also permitted female convicts to be sold openly to settlers and convicts. However, those who met him in Government House society had found him 'indeed quite a man of business and extremely attentive and obliging'.

Due to ill-health he had returned to England in 1804. When Bligh was deposed, he was sailing again for New South Wales, and knew nothing of the rebellion until his arrival. He made his decision to take over the administration before he could possibly have received Bligh's side of the story. In fact, he refused to interview a pro-Bligh deputation sent to greet him. This made him liable for court martial on a charge of mutiny for continuing Bligh's imprisonment. While enjoying his brief rule, Foveaux maintained an impartial attitude towards Bligh and the rebels. The commanding officer of the Corps, William Paterson, remained in Port Dalrymple, Tasmania, where he had been given charge of that small settlement. Foveaux wrote to Paterson in dramatic terms of the state of the colony, which no doubt discouraged Paterson from sailing quickly to take over the administration himself. Paterson was an old veteran; a tired though charming alcoholic, so racked with gout that he could 'hardly withstand a breeze of wind without being affected'. He was in no hurry to investigate the difficult situation in New South Wales.

Foveaux tried to patch up the differences between the rebel factions. Macarthur, who was in one of his black, paranoid rages at being dismissed by Foveaux from the administration, was given the valuable prize of the first land grant within the city of Sydney. But Macarthur was not so easily placated. He later referred to Foveaux as 'that unprincipled man' who had been 'the principal cause of all the mischief that hangs over the colony'.

Foveaux tried very hard to persuade Bligh that, since the HMS *Porpoise* now lay in the harbour, it would be better for everyone concerned if Bligh sailed home to England. But Bligh felt that a Governor could not 'with honor quit his government until he receives permission from his Sovereign'.

Paterson finally faced up to his responsibilities and arrived in Sydney on January 9, 1809. Like Foveaux, he turned a deaf ear to the blusterings of the captive governor, only advising Bligh to return to England. The Rev. Fulton wrote that Paterson was 'almost a paralytic from former intemperance . . . drunk the greatest part of his time; so that from imbecillity when sober and stupidity when drunk, he is a very convenient tool in the hands of McArthur, or of Foveaux and Abbott'. Poor befuddled Paterson would now be held accountable in London for events in the colony, which provided a marvellous opportunity for his advisors—chiefly Foveaux —to embark on a wholesale dispersal of Crown land. During the 12 months when

Paterson was nominally in charge, before the arrival of Macquarie, no less than 67,000 acres were handed out in bribes. The officers of the New South Wales Corps were the main beneficiaries; also the most influential civilian members of the old trading clique, including Simeon Lord, Gregory Blaxland, and Surveyor-General Grimes. Dr Mackaness points out that 19 out of the first 20 men who signed the requisition to Johnston to arrest Bligh received generous tracts of Crown land.

The Rev. Fulton wrote to Mrs Bligh: 'Every spot almost is given away, and the herds of government cattle thinned by gifts of the same kind. Large grants are given to some of the officers of the Corps; if they are removed from this, they intend to leave their families here and return themselves as soon as possible thus to make a powerful party here at all events'.

Mrs Bligh also received a bitter note from Gore: 'Amongst the many extravagant grants bestowed by the rebel government, I neglected mentioning one of 500 acres that has been given to a woman of the name of Nanny Sherwin who cohabits with Foveaux as mistress, it was surveyed on Thursday the 10th of September, in their eagerness to have the grant completed before the troops arrived'. (Once it became known that Macquarie and the 73rd Regiment were on their way to replace the New South Wales Corps, there was a frantic rush to have Paterson's grants surveyed and finalized.) In February, 1809, the captain of HMS *Porpoise* and three of his officers had also received large grants. This was a blatant good-will bribe. Bligh was at this stage playing his last card: he was still legally the naval commandant of all HM ships in the area, and he was trying to exert this authority over the captain and crew of the *Porpoise*.

Paterson forbade Bligh to communicate with the ship, and required him to sign an order directing her to sail to Norfolk Island. Major Johnston and Captain Abbott delivered this message to Bligh at Government House. Bligh wrote: 'I refused to comply with their requisition, when—that their iniquity might be complete—Major Johnston forced me from Government House in a one-horse chaise. He had only drove me two hundred yards when I found my beloved child, under a vertical sun, running after me, having passed Captain Abbott, who told her she need not go, for they would not let her in. Heedless of this, and despising such a want of common feeling of a human being, she got to the barracks when I did, and seizing hold of my arm, we walked into it...' Bligh and Mary Putland were confined in a subaltern's quarters for seven days. Finally he agreed to depart for England on the *Porpoise,* on condition that he would be able to return to Government House before the departure, communicate with his friends, and take with him to England witnesses of his own choice. Bligh pledged that he would proceed to England without touching at any part of the colony. Both sides broke the agreement. First Paterson refused to allow Palmer to accompany Bligh. Then Bligh sailed straight to Van Diemen's land, hoping for active support from the lieutenant-governor at the Derwent, 'Davy' Collins, who had previously expressed sympathy.

Collins at first treated them handsomely, and Mary was installed in a suite at Government House, where, according to Bligh, she was shocked to see Collins 'walking with his kept woman (a poor low creature), arm-in-arm about the town'.

Bligh, however, preferred to sleep on board ship. Relations with Collins became strained when orders from Paterson arrived from Sydney prohibiting the re-victualling of the *Porpoise.* Mary returned on board, and they had to depend for supplies on the captains of ships—whom Bligh ordered alongside—and on a few sympathetic settlers. This ostracism continued for six months. Any other man might have given into his fate long ago, but not Bligh. He seems to have been determined to remain near to New South Wales until relief and instructions arrived from home. In the 20th century it is hard to imagine a situation in which it took six months for a letter to reach England, and another six months to receive a reply. Bligh must have calculated that the serious war at home would mean some further delay in responding to the news of the rebellion, and that the first official report from New South Wales would not have arrived before August or September, 1808. Therefore he could not expect a response in any form before March, 1809, be it an avenging fleet or an official dispatch requiring his return. This was the month in which he had taken the *Porpoise* to Van

Diemen's land. He had no way of knowing—though he must have surmised—that he had been superseded, by the appointment of Nightingall as the future governor in the previous October. He could not have accounted for a further delay of six months—during which Banks exerted pressure for his re-instatement—due to Nightingall's indecision and the unhurried procedure of the Colonial Office. Nor could he have known that the slowness of the response was due in some part to the rumour, somehow planted at the Colonial Office, that he might be already on his way back to England. Though by now, the authorities in London should have known Bligh better than that.

Mary was not well, and the officers of the *Porpoise* were unsympathetic to Bligh, to say the least. The daily hope of some definite news from England was all that kept them going through the hellish nine months of idleness. Collins, not unnaturally, became even more hostile when his son (by his mistress) aged 15 and serving as midshipman on the *Porpoise,* was given the unusually severe punishment of 24 lashes for drunkenness and neglect of duty. Bligh, in his bitterness, had gone too far. The ship had to be moved further down river in response to Collins's threat to fire at any boats attempting to go ashore from her. Relying on his authority as commandant of all ships in the area, Bligh set up a one-man blockade at the mouth of the Derwent where he intercepted shipping for news and supplies. The *Porpoise* sometimes anchored at Adventure Bay which for Bligh was haunted by memories of ships and men from his three previous sojourns here with the *Resolution,* the *Bounty* and the *Providence.* At other times the *Porpoise* lay in the entrance to D'Entrecasteaux Channel at an anchorage known to the locals as 'Bligh's Retreat'. At long last, on December 22, 1809, the storm-battered whaler *Albion* came over the horizon with the news that a new governor had sailed for New South Wales many months ago. On New Year's Day, as Macquarie formally took office in Sydney, the leaky old *Porpoise* slipped out of the Derwent bound for Sydney.

CHAPTER XV

Trial
and Death

On January 16, 1810, Macquarie greeted Bligh's return to New South Wales with every mark of honour. But, as Bligh sized up the new situation, he was not pleased. He had presumed that the rebels remaining in the colony would be brought to justice, and that the loyalists who had suffered on his behalf would be acknowledged and rewarded. Johnston and Macarthur had departed for England, and Macquarie's policy was conciliatory. Bligh noted that the principal supporters of the rebellion were frequent guests at Government House, that some were still in official positions, and that Foveaux was Macquarie's chief confidant. And the new Judge-Advocate—for at last Bligh's requests for a competent successor to Atkins had been heeded—decided that rebels in the colony would not be tried until further advice had been received from Britain.

Macquarie believed that there had been no excuse for the mutiny against Bligh: 'very few complaints having been made to me against him, and even those few are rather of a trifling nature'. Bligh stayed on in Sydney for four months, collecting several witnesses to accompany him to London for the trial of Johnston, and assembling evidence. By March, Macquarie was complaining to his brother that Bligh was 'a great plague' to him, 'a most disagreeable Person to have any dealings, or Publick business to transact with', and that he would be 'heartily glad to get quit of him'. Bligh's letter to his wife in the same month explains why he and Macquarie were not the best of friends. 'The loyal persons are the least attended to; Foveaux is in power and the New South Wales Corps doing duty here in great glee, while the 73rd is encamped 2 miles out of town—Visiting between the parties are as common as if nothing had happened, and altho Governor Macquarie and ourselves are on good terms, yet we cannot account for such phenomena, and particularly as we will not dine with any of them at Government House. All we do is to act with mildness and avoid any altercation or appearance of displeasure... It is a hard trial of my temper to be here just now, to see all the poor loyalists in the background: however, my arrival will, I hope, tend to their advantage and I have the greatest comfort and happy reflections on the good I have done the Country and the hereafter benefits which will be derived from my conduct.'

Bligh could be very pompous when his spirits were at a low ebb, but this was no hollow boast. He had, through his courage and stubbornness, acted as a catalyst in the affairs of the colony. The rebellion brought nothing but personal tragedy to Bligh, but it made the task of governing much easier for his successor. The power of the avaricious trading group was broken and Macarthur could not return to plague Macquarie for nearly a decade. The inglorious New South Wales Corps was recalled, and justice, in the person of a competent new Judge-Advocate, could now be expected to prevail in the courts. Macquarie was able to continue Bligh's policy of encouraging small settlers and worthy emancipists for many years, until Britain, with an eye on wool and profits, abandoned the original idealistic master-plan for the colony.

On the eve of Bligh's departure for England, fate struck him another blow. His 'beloved Mary', his most loyal supporter, announced her marriage to Lieutenant-Colonel O'Connell of the 73rd. Bligh hated to leave her behind— only a few weeks before he had written to his wife: 'All my endeavours are to keep up our Dear Mary's health and spirits and the idea of my restoring her to you and Her Dear Sisters keep up mine'. Now he had to write from Rio of the new turn of events, with very mixed emotions: 'In the highest feelings of comfort and pride of bringing her to England, altho I thought she could be under no guidance but my own—my heart devoted to her—in the midst of most parental affections and conflicting passions of adoration for so good and admired child, I at the last found what I had the least expected—Lieut. Col. O'Connel commanding the 73rd Regt. had unknown to me won her affections. Nothing can exceed the esteem and high character he has. He is likewise Lt Govr of the Territory... What will you not my dear Betsy feel for my situation at the time, when you know that nothing I could say had any effect: at last overwhelmed with a loss I could not retrieve, I had only to make the best of it... Thus my Dear Love, when I thought nothing could have induced our dear child to have quitted me, have I left her behind in the finest climate in the World, which to have taken her from into the tempestuous voyage I have performed I now believe would have caused her death'.

Bligh seemed always quite blind to the workings of human emotion. But at least he was pleased by her wedding and 'the admiration and respect of Govr and Mrs Macquarrie, who did the honors of the ceremony at Government House with an extraordinary degree of pleasure'.

Meanwhile, the rebel party in London was busy mustering all possible influence for the coming legal battle. Johnston was fortunate enough to have the patronage of the Duke of Northumberland, and when he and Macarthur arrived in October 1809 they were received by the Duke 'on the terms of closest friendship'. (The Duke was related to the military secretary of the Commander-in-Chief of the army, the Duke of York.) Macarthur came bearing gifts: two emus were bestowed on Lady Castlereagh, and Lady Camden was delighted to receive a swan and a goose. An additional bonus of bronze-wing pigeons was considered by Macarthur, but he was advised that 'so many presents at one time would overdo the business'. Presumably, further favours were held in reserve—one never knew what the future might bring. 'Lord Camden', Macarthur informed his wife, 'continues President of the Council—of course I cannot expect to be received by him until matters are settled, but I have good reason to think he is well inclined towards me.'

Bligh arrived on October 25, 1810; apparently unencumbered by presents save some 'Gold Beads in strings' and 'Six handsome Crosses' for his wife and the 'Dear Girls'. Sir Joseph Banks and the Rev. Samuel Marsden had been outspoken on his behalf. Marsden was the chaplain of the colony, and though he had been absent at the time of the rebellion, he was able to inform those who had ears to listen about the state of New South Wales and the character of the rebels. Macarthur raged that he was 'propagating the most diabolical falsehoods for the purpose of creating favourable opinions of the virtues of his friend Bligh and his party, whilst, on the other hand, he has blackened the character of myself and the opponents of Bligh by the most scandalous reports'. Still, Marsden was somewhat remote from the corridors of power. Late in 1810 Macarthur was able to report with satisfaction: 'I have found a powerful body of friends in this country, who are not only able but willing to give me their support to my endeavours to obtain satisfaction for the past and security for the future'. At this stage, Johnston and Macarthur, working on the theory that attack is the best means of defence, planned a civil action against Bligh with damages laid at £20,000. However, this audacious plan failed. Johnston was to be court martialled.

The trial did not take place until May 7, 1811. The hearing lasted for 13 days. The charge against Johnston was mutiny, and there were 23 witnesses for the prosecution and 19 for the defence. Since the fact of mutiny could hardly be disputed, the only line of defence open to Johnston lay in showing that the mutiny was justified by an extreme state of emergency in the colony; that Bligh had to be arrested for his own safety and the safety of the public. This involved proving that Bligh was so feared and hated during a lawless and tyrannical regime that only his deposition prevented a general insurrection. In other words, Bligh was on trial, too.

Fortunately, Bligh had engaged an excellent attorney; a man who was to have a brilliant career, now known as plain Mr Frederick Pollock, later as Lord Chief Baron Pollock. Moreover, Bligh was very able in his own defence; and on the whole the calibre of his witnesses—men like Campbell, Palmer, Fulton, Gore and George Suttor—was decidedly more impressive than that of the opposition team which starred Macarthur, Captain Fenn Kemp, Lieutenant Minchin, John Blaxland, Dr Harris and four soldiers from the New South Wales Corps.

'The soldiers gave the most atrocious falsehoods in proof of my arbitrary character', wrote Bligh to Banks during the course of the trial, 'and stuck at nothing to lessen Johnston's guilt. One of the soldiers, a sergeant-major, when in the midst of his zeal and falsehood against me, was suddenly seized with a fainting fit like the stroke of death and was taken out of court.' Of Minchin, Bligh wrote: 'Two particular instances Minchin described with all the appearance of truth, but my fortunately having the minute of the proceedings of the Court, it turned everything against him and proved he was the most competent false witness that ever existed to the great abhorrence of everyone present'. And Kemp 'stuck at nothing but at last the Court brought him to say that he spoke only from hearsay'.

Other witnesses for the defence fared little better. Dr Harris, for instance, claimed that a major cause of dissatisfaction had been Bligh's order that stray dogs should be shot. This was a silly statement in the first place—Sydney residents had often complained about the dangerous packs of starving curs which kept them awake at nights and attacked them by day. But it was made even more absurd when Bligh managed to produce a copy of the Sydney Gazette in which Harris had advertised: 'any dogs hereafter found within Mr Harris' enclosure will be shot and the

Private seal belonging to Bligh.

owners prosecuted in case of damage'.

Macarthur himself, in spite of all the expertise acquired in his colonial litigations, failed to perform well. His rhetorical flights tended to be pinned-down and deflated. At one point, the Judge-Advocate himself, tired of hearing of Macarthur's 'dread' of an 'insurrection', cut in sharply to say: 'It seems the first cause of grievance was the detention of that ship of yours, and the forfeiture of the bond for £900; the next is about a post that was taken away from your ground; and these seem to have been the principal part of all the causes of the revolution'.

Though in one sense the trial went well for Bligh, the evidence against him—both false and true—was a daily humiliation. It did emerge that, if not an unfit man to be a governor, he was not fit to govern New South Wales at that time. He had indeed been at times unnecessarily over-bearing, high-handed and violent in humour and language, though,

given the tactics of the opposition, this was not surprising. In fact there were some who believed that Macarthur had planned to get rid of Bligh by a strategy of defiance from the very start of his governorship. The Rev. Fulton had written to Castlereagh: 'From the time of his arrival in the colony, and even before it, he has been traduced as a tyrant. In a secret and designing manner, McArthur pretended that he had a very gloomy prospect with respect to Governor Bligh's reign, as he called it. When the General Orders were issued prohibiting the barter of spirits, Mr McArthur said...that the licensed retailers of spirits... would have all the money in the colony, and that the soldiers would not suffer it'.

At the trial, a Captain Walker recalled that Macarthur had told him that: 'Gov. Bligh was giving the Government property to the settlers, a set of rascals who would deceive him; it would be better if he gave it to me and some of the other respectable gentlemen of the colony; if he does not, he will perhaps get another voyage in his launch again'. Many other hints point to the conclusion that the rebellion had been planned for a long time before it occurred, if not in the exact form in which it took place. Certainly Macarthur provoked Bligh deliberately in the final showdowns, and Dr Evatt, in his *Rum Rebellion*, shows that there was collusion between Macarthur, Johnston and Abbott some days before the rebellion was staged.

On July 2 the verdict of the court martial was announced: Johnston was guilty of the charge of mutiny. As punishment, he was merely cashiered out of the army. The Prince Regent, acting for the King, commented that the sentence had been so inadequate that the Court had apparently taken into consideration the 'novel and extraordinary circumstances' which appeared to have existed during Bligh's administration. No doubt the court was reluctant to act against a man who was in reality Macarthur's tool. Even so, Johnston had a narrow escape—one member of the court martial told Macquarie later that, through illness, he had been unable to attend the court on the day that sentence was passed: 'This I believe was very fortunate for Johnston for I never heard as connected an evidence proving him guilty of mutiny—without the least palliation that was in my mind worthy of consideration'.

Johnston returned to New South Wales in a ship loaded with his merchandise and livestock. Macquarie granted him more land to add to his already large property at Annandale, where he retired in comfort.

Macarthur was unable to return to New South Wales for another eight years. As a civilian he could not be tried in London, but Macquarie was still under orders from the Secretary of State to arrest him if he should return to New South Wales. Until this instruction was withdrawn, his wife ran his estates while he fretted in London and brooded on his enemies.

It was considered unnecessary to take action against other rebels, especially as the Corps had now left the colony forever. Foveaux breathed a sigh of relief. Paterson and Collins were both now dead anyway.

Bligh wrote in disgust to his nephew: 'You will observe the severe censure the Prince throws on the Members of the Court which was all he could do & I believe that Johnston only escaped death through the means of the Northumberland interest—it is certainly unjust proceedings—he had no Witness but those who were concerned in the Mutiny and rebellion. While mine were all loyal People— only half however were called on & those not asked half the Questions that were necessary for the l. Ad. General commanded the Court & did all—& he was in the Northumberland interest—I was confined to the Charge of Mutiny... When I can inform you of the whole proceedings—& you know the veneration I was held in by the whole of the Colony, you will be astonished beyond belief'.

Poor Bligh survived the humiliations and slander, but his wife did not. In November, he wrote to his nephew that she was dangerously ill. After becoming too weak to stand or eat, she died on April 15, 1812, in her sixtieth year. Pollock, the lawyer, reminisced many years later how, during and after the trial, Bligh and Mrs Bligh 'and indeed all the family, became my intimate friends. Mrs Bligh did not long survive the anxiety she had endured while his promotion was stopped, his pension suspended and his conduct impeached'.

Bligh was promoted to rear-admiral of the Blue Squadron as soon as the trial was over. But he was now 58 and did not see active service again. In 1813 he was granted the pension which had been promised him as Governor, and he sold his London house and retired to a fine manor house in Kent with his four unmarried daughters, where they admired the corn and hops.

In 1814 he became vice-admiral of the Blue. In 1812 he had been called upon to give evidence and advice to the Select Committee of the House of Commons on the transportation of convicts to New South Wales, and in 1814 the Admiralty commissioned him to join a committee of six naval experts to report on a plan for a new 74-gun ship. It was an honourable retirement—as Dr Mackaness said, he was held in high esteem among his friends in England, having, in his domestic affairs, 'worn the white flower of a blameless moral life' in an age when drunkenness and adultery were the common vices of a gentleman.

In 1817, some internal disorder—probably cancer—sent him frequently up to London for treatment, and on one of these visits, on December 7, he died.

He was buried beside his wife in the churchyard of St. Mary's, Lambeth. His estate was left to his six daughters. The youngest, Elizabeth, married a cousin, Richard Bligh. The twins, with poor Anne, moved to Notting Hill—all three lived to a ripe old age. Each of the three married daughters named a son after her father.

His peaceful decline is in strange contrast to the deaths of his greatest adversaries—the *Bounty* mutineers who succumbed to murder or alcohol on their island, and John Macarthur, who succumbed to his own full-blown paranoia.

George Tobin, the artist who sailed with Bligh, made an apt and just assessment of the man: 'So poor Bligh, for with all his infirmities, you and I cannot but think well of him, has followed Portlock. He has had a long and turbulent journey of it—no one more so, and since the unfortunate Mutiny in the *Bounty,* has been rather in the shade. Yet perhaps was he not altogether understood—I am sure, my dear Friend that in the *Providence* there was no settled System of Tyranny exercised by him likely to produce dissatisfaction. It was in those violent Tornados of temper when he lost himself, yet, when all, in his opinion, went right, when could a man be more placid and interesting. For myself I feel that I am indebted to him ... Once or twice I felt the Unbridled licence of his power of speech, yet never without soon receiving something like an emollient plaister to heal the wound. Let our old Captain's frailties be forgotten and view him as a man of Science and excellent practical Seaman. He had suffered much and even in difficulty by labour and perseverance extricated himself'.

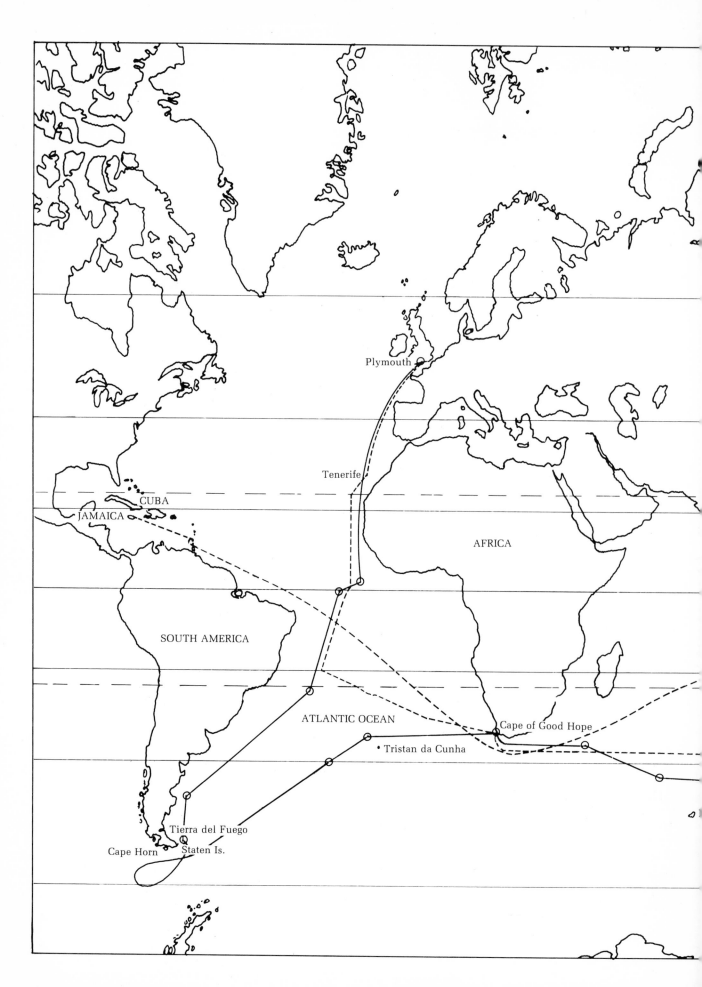

Plymouth

Tenerife

CUBA

JAMAICA

AFRICA

SOUTH AMERICA

ATLANTIC OCEAN

Cape of Good Hope

• Tristan da Cunha

Tierra del Fuego

Cape Horn   Staten Is.

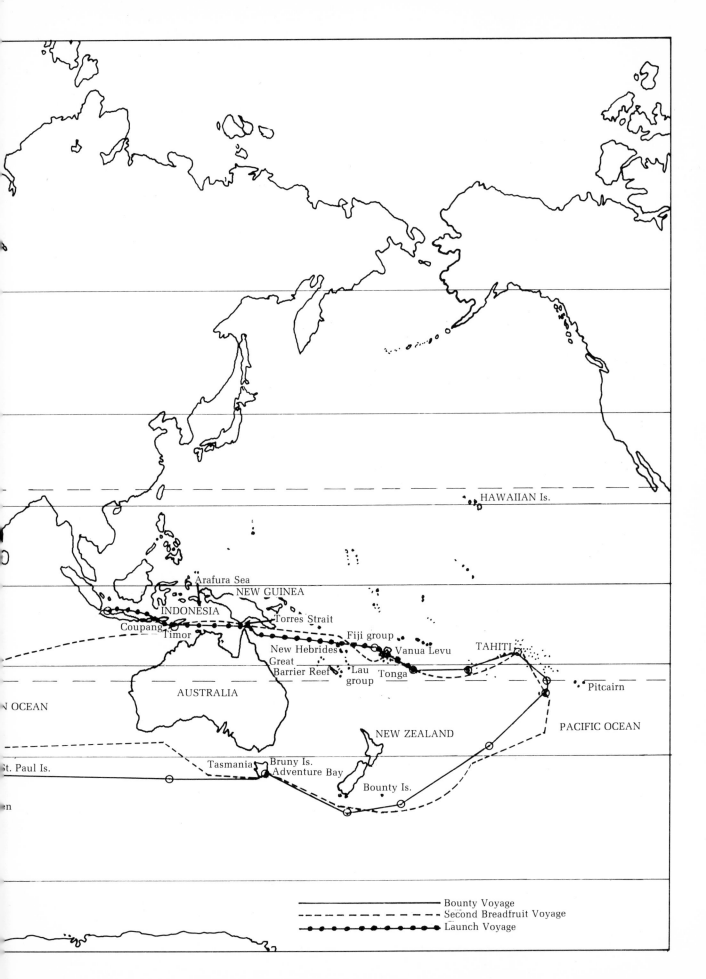

Arafura Sea
NEW GUINEA
INDONESIA
Coupang
Timor
Torres Strait
Fiji group
New Hebrides
Vanua Levu
TAHITI
Great
Barrier Reef
Lau
group
Tonga
Pitcairn
AUSTRALIA
OCEAN
NEW ZEALAND
PACIFIC OCEAN
St. Paul Is.
Tasmania
Bruny Is.
Adventure Bay
Bounty Is.

HAWAIIAN Is.

———————————— Bounty Voyage
- - - - - - - - - - - Second Breadfruit Voyage
●●●●●●●●●●●●● Launch Voyage

Acknowledgements

The publisher wishes to thank the following for their assistance and co-operation in the making of this book:

Mitchell Library
Institute of Jamaica
British Museum
National Maritime Museum
Auckland Star
National Library of Australia (Rex Nan Kivell Coll.)
Dixson Galleries
National Portrait Gallery
Alexander Turnbull Library
Public Library of N.S.W.
Rex Reinits Estate
Dan O'Keefe
Pioneers Club
Geelong Art Gallery

The authors are grateful to the Mitchell Library, Sydney, for their assistance in supplying vital manuscript sources.

Selected Reading List
Dugan, J., *The Great Mutiny,* Andre Deutsch, London, 1966.
Ellis, M. H., *John Macarthur,* Angus & Robertson, Sydney, 1958.
Ellis, M. H., *Lachlan Macquarie,* Angus & Robertson, Sydney, 1947.
Evatt, H. V., *Rum Rebellion,* Angus & Robertson, Sydney, 1938.
Lewis, M., *A Social History of the Navy, 1793-1815,* London, 1960.
Lloyd, C., *The British Seaman,* Collins, London, 1968.
Mackaness, G., *The Life of Vice-Admiral William Bligh,* Angus & Robertson, London, 1951.

Index

SACRED
TO THE MEMORY OF
WILLIAM BLIGH. ESQUIRE. F.R.S.
VICE ADMIRAL OF THE BLUE.
THE CELEBRATED NAVIGATOR
WHO FIRST TRANSPLANTED THE BREAD FRUIT TREE
FROM OTAHEITE TO THE WEST INDIES,
BRAVELY FOUGHT THE BATTLES OF HIS COUNTRY
AND DIED BELOVED, RESPECTED. AND LAMENTED.
ON THE 7TH DAY OF DECEMBER. 1817.
AGED 64.